AN INDEX OF CHARACTERS
IN ENGLISH PRINTED DRAMA
TO THE RESTORATION

By Thomas L. Berger
and
William C. Bradford, Jr.

1975

Microcard Editions Books
An Indian Head Company
A Division of Information Handling Services

Published by Microcard Editions Books
P.O. Box 1154
Englewood, Colorado 80110

Printed in the United States of America

Cover art by Barbara B. Anderson

FOR

GEORGE WALTON WILLIAMS

CONTENTS

Section I
Introduction

A lengthy introductory statement to a work such as this may seem inappropriate, but we would like to be certain that our readers understand the nature of our intentions for the book and of our attempts to be as inclusive as is practical. The need for an index of characters in Renaissance drama first came to our attention several years ago when we sought, unaware of our independent quests, a work which would list all Renaissance plays in which Julius Caesar and Lazarillo de Tormes appear. Finding none, Berger approached Bradford with the suggestion that we compile one, and, totally ignorant of the complexities involved, we innocently began. Over the years, the necessity of setting some guidelines about the characters we would include and exclude became increasingly apparent; our methods have, as a result, been altered and refined numerous times. We speak here of our methods and of some of the problems we encountered with the hope that we may facilitate the use of our book.

The index includes all of the characters who appear in the English printed drama of the Tudor, Elizabethan, Jacobean, Caroline, and Commonwealth ages; our primary sources have been the English plays listed in W. W. Greg's *Bibliography of English Printed Drama to the Restoration*.[1] The method used to index the characters in these plays has been relatively simple. Each of us read the first edition of each play listed by Greg and other sixteenth- and seventeenth-century editions of that play whenever Greg indicates that it possesses substantive variants of the nature we sought. We then checked our reading against a modern edition of the play (if it existed) and against extant manuscript versions of the play (whenever they were accessible) or against modern editions of the play which list manuscript variants. From our reading, we compiled a complete Dramatis Personae for each play.

Each character has his own entry in the index, followed by the numbers (Greg's) of the plays in which he appears;[2] in most instances, he has several entries in the index. In addition

---

[1] 4 vols. (London: The Bibliographical Society, 1939–57). We do not deal with plays in manuscript (Thomas Middleton's *The Witch*, for example), with printed Latin plays (Greg, II, L 1–L 23), with lost plays, some of whose characters are known or at least suggested (Greg, II, Θ 1–Θ 187), or with English printed plays not included in Greg's *Bibliography (The Welcome for Philip and Mary*, a pageant printed about 1555, and *The King Found at Southwell*, an entertainment of 1646, are but two examples). This final class of plays with which we do not deal awaits bibliographical classification in Greg's system.

[2] A Finding List follows the index.

to the entries for his given name and for his surname, he may have an entry for his nationality, occupation, religious proclivity, and/or his psychological state if any or all of these are mentioned in the text of the play (either in the Dramatis Personae, in the dialogue of the play, or in stage directions), in a critical study of the play, or in a modern study of character types, nationalities, or occupations as they were represented in Renaissance plays.[3] All such names and identifying characteristics we list separately. For example, if a play were to include a character named John Smith who is a melancholic Puritan carpenter of Islington, this character would appear six times in the index, under JOHN, SMITH, MELANCHOLIC(S), PURITAN(S), CARPENTER(S), and ISLINGTON. Exigencies of space preclude our indexing this John Smith separately under SMITH, JOHN as well as under his given and his surname; no named character is so listed.

Even plays which had a single edition present problems, both with regard to the names of characters and to their nationalities. Obvious misprints in names we have corrected, but in our desire to be as inclusive as possible, we have chosen to index all substantive and semi-substantive variants in the spellings of names. In Ralph Knevet's *Rhodon and Iris* (1631; Greg no. 449; STC 15036),[4] for example, the Dramatis Personae lists ADANTHUS as a character, while throughout the text itself, the character ACANTHUS appears. We retain ACANTHUS and omit ADANTHUS. The same kind of problem exists with the character CYNOBASTUS in the same play; we have omitted the incorrect listing of CYNOBATUS given in the Dramatis Personae. Similarly, in Robert Daborne's *The Poor Man's Comfort* (1617; Greg no. 741; STC D101), LICURGO and GLISCO appear throughout the text; we omit the LITTIGO and GLISTAR of the Dramatis Personae. On the other hand, in the first and only seventeenth-century edition of James Shirley's *The Example* (1634; Greg no. 521; STC 22442), the character FITZAVARICE appears one time as FITZAMOROUS and is often corrected (in a seventeenth-century hand) in the University of Michigan's copy of the quarto to FITZAMOROUS. In this instance, we have chosen to index both names. A similar dilemma occurs in another play by Shirley, *The Ball* (1632; Greg no. 549; STC 4995); here, the spellings SENTILLA and SCUTILLA, referring to the same character, appear with equal frequency. We index both names for this character, as we do with NEOPHILUS and NEOPHITUS in the anonymous *Nero* (1624; Greg no. 410; STC 18430). With the designation of nationalities, inconsistencies frequently appear in quartos. The Dramatis Personae of Shakerley Marmion's *The Antiquary* (1635; Greg no. 601; STC M703) indicates that the play is set in Pisa and that the Duke is of that city. The text of the play reveals, however, that the setting is Venice. We index both PISA and VENICE, for at one time Pisa may have been important in the composition of the play. The Venetian setting for John Fletcher's *The Captain* (1612; Greg no. 642; STC B1581) presents a similar problem. Though the first edition specifies no particular setting, the folio edition of 1679 lists both Venice and Spain; we include both VENETIAN(S) and SPANIARD(S) for this play.

Plays with two or more substantively different texts, unfinished printed plays, and plays with more than one edition or with a manuscript version provide distinct problems, some rather troublesome, others less severe though worthy of mention. *Hamlet* (1601; Greg no. 197; STC 22275), always an enigma to scholars and critics, has proven no less a one to us. We have chosen to index all those characters in Q1 whose names are changed in subsequent editions; of course, we also index the more familiar names of the subsequent editions. Thus, CORAMBIS (Polonius' name in Q1) has an entry in the index, as do ALBERTUS, VOLTEMAR, and MONTANO, the names assigned by the bad quarto to the

---

[3]See our Bibliography for a list of works consulted.

[4]The date we give here and after every title is the date of first performance, as in Alfred Harbage, *Annals of English Drama, 975–1700*, revised by Samuel Schoenbaum (Philadelphia: University of Pennsylvania Press, 1964) or in Schoenbaum's supplements to this book.

more recognizable GONZAGO, VOLTEMAND, and REYNALDO. Similarly, the first edition of Ben Jonson's *Every Man in his Humour* (1598; Greg no. 176; STC 14766) sets the play in Florence; the folio text of 1616 moves the setting to London and renames many of the characters to suit the change in setting.[5] We index the characters from both versions of the play, as we do for Richard Flecknoe's *Love's Dominion,* or, as he later entitled it, *Love's Kingdom* (1654; Greg no. 738; STC F1228).[6] The text of Jonson's incomplete *Mortimer his Fall* (1637; Greg no. 615; STC 14754) presents only MORTIMER (Earl of MARCH) and ISABEL, though the Dramatis Personae lists twenty-one other possible entries; we have chosen to index all twenty-four characters. The 1673 folio edition of William Davenant's *Works* necessitates three additional entries for *The Unfortunate Lovers* (1638; Greg no. 624; STC D348); the folio adds the characters ORNA and PHOEBE to the Dramatis Personae as it appeared in the first edition and changes FRISKIN's name to FRISKLIN. In Q1 of the anonymous *Wine, Beer, Ale, and Tobacco* (1625; Greg no. 426; STC 11541), the character TOBACCO is mentioned but does not appear; his inclusion in the second edition of the play requires that he be indexed. Sometimes, later editions and/or manuscript versions of plays require the inclusion in our index of additional entries. The 1674 edition of Jonson's *Works* adds a PROLOGUE to *Cataline his Conspiracy* (1611; Greg no. 296; STC 14759), and the manuscript in the British Museum of Milton's *The Masque at Ludlow Castle* (1634; Greg no. 524; STC 17937) includes a PROLOGUE to the piece, composed of lines 975–82, 987–94, 994A, 995, and 997–98 from the first edition. The Bodleian manuscript of the anonymous *Pathomachia* (1617; Greg no. 434; STC 19462) calls for the addition of more than seventy entries to the index for a single character. For URBANITY's reading of the list of PRIDE's names in IV.iv, the compositor was only willing to print URBANITY's words as "Sir Antoniastro-Adriano-Alexandrino; Sir Bellarmino-Baronia-Bombo, etc.," but the manuscript provides the complete list and serves as an explanation for the compositor's reluctance. The manuscript extends URBANITY's speech to:

> Sir Belialo Bezeco Belzebub. Sir Caligula Caracalla Came. Sir Diastrophe Dioclesiano Decio. Sir Exuperantio, Eldorada Embrodarara: Sir Ferdinando Firifacio. Hiflappo. Sir Gregoriano Guilt spurratho-Galligasken. Sir Heildebrando, Hispanioso-Hitchmctaile. Sir Juliano Jebusita Jambres. Sir Knioleflanko Kappuchino koriato knaueingrane. Sir Lucianissimo. Luciferiano Lickfame: Sir Moloniano Marprelate Molthorse. Sir Neronanello Nebuchodonozoro-Nimrod. Sir Octaviano-opobalsamo-owennist. Sir Peirpaul-Puritano-Paracelso. Sir Quarrellado-quelquechose-quaintguilt. Sir Roderigo Riotossa Roaringboy. Sir Sennacheribo, Saladino, Speakbig. Sir Tully Tarquin-Traiano-Tamberlain. Sir Uselesse-Viperado-Verpendragon. Sir Widemouth-Wonderosa-Wilderim. Sir xenophon romastigo-Xerxadoro-Xileno. Sir Yield to none yea my Lord Yawnell. Sir Zealamimo-Zanzummim-Zanie.

Modern editions of Renaissance plays frequently make emendations of characters' names that are significant enough to merit inclusion in the index. Most modern editors omit from the first scene of *2 Henry the Fourth* (1597; Greg no. 167; STC 22288) the name Sir John Umfreville; soon after his entrance and ever after, he is called Lord Bardolph. We index JOHN, UMFREVILLE, and BARDOLPH, just as we include CLAUDIO and VARRUS from the F1 text of Shakespeare's *Julius Caesar* (1599; Greg no. 403; STC 22273), even though subsequent editors have changed their names to CLAUDIUS and VARRO.

---

[5]J. W. Lever discusses these alterations in his edition of the play (Lincoln: University of Nebraska Press, 1971).

[6]Since Flecknoe's play had failed in 1654, he decided to bring out a second "edition" in 1664. He explained in his Epistle Dedicatory that "the People . . . condemn'd this Play on the Stage, for want of being rightly represented unto them"; as a result, he declared that "unless it may be presented as I writ it, and as I intended it, I had rather it shu'd be read than acted" (Sig. A2). For this "reader's" edition, Flecknoe changed the names of some of his characters.

Though H. H. Wood, in his edition of Marston's *Histriomastix* (1599; Greg no. 290; STC 13529), emends the RUFFETINGS of Q1 to RUSSETINGS,[7] we include both character types in our index, and, in a similar way, we enter SEMUS as his name appears in the first two quartos of Middleton's *A Mad World my Masters* (1606; Greg no. 276; STC 17888), even though a recent editor has decided that his name is a misprint for SERVUS.[8] A typical example of the kinds of vexations we faced when confronted with some editors' emendations (no matter how reasonable those emendations may be) is evident in Norman Sanders' edition of Robert Greene's *James the Fourth* (1590; Greg no. 149; STC 12308). We index the character OLIVE PAT, in spite of Sanders' suggestion that "Olive Pat" is a part of a description in a stage direction. The corrected quarto of the play reads:

> *Enter* Cirus *King, humbling themselues: himselfe crowned*
> *by* Oliue *Pat, at last dying, layde in a*
> *marbell tombe with this inscription.* . . .

Sanders emends the stage direction to read:

> *Enter* Cyrus, *Kings humbling themselves; himself crowned*
> *by olive, that at last dying [is] laid in a*
> *marble tomb with this inscription.* . . .[9]

In addition to the decisions we had to make with regard to the various editions of individual plays, we were forced to confront problems of differing kinds within the texts of the plays themselves. Our intent is to include all characters who appear on stage, even if a character does not appear alive, all in one piece, or as himself. For Shakespeare's *Richard the Third* (1593; Greg no. 142; STC 22314), for example, we have included HENRY VI OF ENGLAND since his corpse is carried on stage in the opening act.[10] And, for *Measure for Measure* (1604; Greg no. 392; STC 22273), we index RAGOZINE, BOHEMIA, his native country, and his occupation, PIRATE, for it is his head that is substituted for Julio's in the closing act of the play.[11] For disguised characters we enter their real names *and* the names they assume. GANYMEDE and ALIENA, the disguises assumed by ROSALIND and CELIA in *As You Like It* (1599; Greg no. 394; STC 22273), are included along with their real names, as are CAESARIO (VIOLA) and Sir TOPAS (FESTE) from *Twelfth Night or What you Will* (1600; Greg no. 396; STC 22273), BELLARIO (EUPHRASIA) from Beaumont and Fletcher's *Philaster* (1609; Greg no. 363; STC 1681), THALESTRIS (SPACONIA) from their *A King and no King* (1611; Greg no. 360; STC 1670), and any number of other aliases we could list here.

It is often difficult to determine whether or not some named characters actually appear, but we have tried to be consistent in our inclusions by interpreting stage directions. In *Measure for Measure*, for instance, we assume that the "Lords" who come on stage at the beginning of Act V are the same ones called for in IV.v.6–10 and named there as VALENTINUS, CRASSUS, ROWLAND, and FLAVIUS; we feel justified, therefore, in our attempts to be as inclusive as possible, in entering these names in the index. In the same

---

[7]*The Plays of John Marston*, III (Edinburgh: Oliver and Boyd, 1939).

[8]Standish Hennig, ed. (Lincoln: University of Nebraska Press, 1965).

[9]*The Scottish History of James the Fourth* (Cambridge: Harvard University Press, 1970), pp. 130–31.

[10]Other corpses abound: in Thomas May's *Antigone* (1627; Greg no. 450; STC 17716), Polynices' body is carried on stage; in Thomas Drue's *The Duchess of Suffolk* (1624; Greg no. 451; STC 7242), Vandermast's body is present; and in John Kirke's *The Seven Champions of Christendom* (1635; Greg no. 545; STC 15014), the corpse of Prince Arbasto is briefly seen.

[11]Other named heads we index too: Proculus' head appears in the anonymous *Nero* (1624; Greg no. 410; STC 18430), as does Lollia Paulina's in Thomas May's *Julia Agrippina* (1628; Greg no. 554; STC 17718).

way, we index the Iberian Captains ZENON and EVARNESS from J.S.'s *Andromana* (1642; Greg no. 813; STC S3459), for though they are only mentioned in the text as participating in the battle against the Argives, they are probably among those "captains" who enter later in the play. Also, when the BAWD in Thomas Heywood's *The Royal King and the Loyal Subject* (1602; Greg no. 516; STC 13364) calls on F2^v for her whores SIS, JOYCE, and PRISCILLA, and when "2 wenches enter with 2 gentlemen" on the following page, we assume that these two wenches possess two of the three names mentioned earlier; since we cannot know which two, we index all three names, as well as WHORE(S) and WENCH(ES). In a related kind of decision, we chose to exclude the fourteen named characters in the anonymous *The Kentish Fair* (1648; Greg no. 674.5; STC K324), for they are mentioned as being just off stage but do not appear or speak.

We have included all animals appearing in the plays as well as inanimate objects whose roles are taken by actors. The dogs CRAB (from *The Two Gentlemen of Verona* [1593; Greg no. 391; STC 22273]), FURY, SILVER, MOUNTAIN, and TYRANT (from *The Tempest* [1611; Greg no. 390; STC 22273]) are all indexed, as is the BEAR that pursues Antigonus in *The Winter's Tale* (1610; Greg no. 397; STC 22273). Since IO becomes a COW in Thomas Heywood's *Jupiter and Io* (1635; Greg no. 528; STC 13358), we feel obligated to include IO in her bovine state. Among the other animals we index are the APE(S) in James Shirley's *Cupid and Death* (1653; Greg no. 713; STC S3464) and the BIRD(S) in Shirley's *The Triumph of Peace* (1634; Greg no. 488; STC 22459)—a MAGPIE, a CROW, a JAY, a KITE, and an OWL. Since we feel it wrong to eliminate Snout's WALL or Starveling's MOONSHINE from *A Midsummer-Night's Dream* (1595; Greg no. 170; STC 22302), we have also included such inanimate objects as the WINDMILL in Shirley's *The Triumph of Peace*, the BOTTLE(S), TUN(S), and BARREL(S) of Ben Jonson's *Pleasure Reconciled to Virtue* (1618; Greg no. 608; STC 14754), and the living STATUE(S) who appear in Francis Beaumont's *The Masque of the Inner Temple and Gray's Inn* (1613; Greg no. 309; STC 1663), in Thomas Campion's *The Lord's Masque* (1613; Greg no. 319; STC 4545), and in *The Winter's Tale*.

So called "ghost" characters, characters who may have one name in the Dramatis Personae and another in the text of the play or characters who may be listed in the Dramatis Personae and appear nowhere in the text, present special problems. We index them, since at some time in the process of composition, they may have been important to the playwright in his conception of the play. For this reason, we include INNOGEN, the "ghost" character in *Much Ado about Nothing* (1598; Greg no. 168; STC 22304),[12] and MANDANE in Beaumont and Fletcher's *A King and no King*. The Marshal's daughter in Thomas Heywood's *The Royal King and the Loyal Subject* is called MARGARET in the Dramatis Personae of the play but has the name KATHERINE in the text; we index both names for this one character. The inner forme of sheet F of Thomas Dekker's *Match me in London* (1611; Greg no. 440; STC 6529) exists in three states. On the first uncorrected sheet appears a "ghost" character named FARENTES, but on the corrected sheet, he is called FUENTES; here, too, we index both names.

Character types and nationalities constitute two classes of characters whose inclusion in the index is essential and easy to justify but, nonetheless, frequently difficult to classify. In the plays under consideration, therefore, there are most certainly more CON-SPIRATOR(S), FAVORITE(S), MURDERER(S), USURPER(S), VILLAIN(S), and VIRGIN(S) than we list. We have chosen to include such character types in the index only when they are named in either the text of the play or in a modern study of the type on the

---

[12]W. W. Greg discusses the nature of "ghost" characters in Shakespeare in *The Shakespeare First Folio* (Oxford: Clarendon Press, 1955), pp. 112, 195.

Renaissance stage. Our listing for TYRANT(S), for example, relies on the texts of the plays themselves and on an article by W.A. Armstrong.[13] The same criterion applies to POISONER(S), PROSTITUTE(S), and PURITAN(S),[14] and there are surely more MASKER(S) than those we include, for our list has been compiled from those characters called MASKER(S) in the texts we examined and so described by Ewbank.[15] Similarly, we are certain that there are more LONDONER(S) in Renaissance plays than the ones we have indexed. Nor have we included all the GREEK(S) or ROMAN(S) in those plays set in the classical past; playwrights had every reason to count on their audiences knowing that AGAMEMNON was a GREEK and that CAESAR was a ROMAN, and they more often than not excluded nationalistic designations in their descriptions of such characters. Our general rule, once again, has been to include such nationalities only when they are used by the playwright or pointed out in a modern study of the nationality in Renaissance plays.[16] On the other hand, we probably have included more JEW(S) in our index than there actually were in the plays, for some studies of the Jew in English literature designate as a Jew almost any character who only might have been considered Jewish.[17]

If we have inadvertently omitted some characters who probably could have been indexed, we have intentionally left out several kinds of characters that we feel have to be excluded for reasons of space in the index or for more specific reasons. Nearly every play has one or all of the following characters: SERVANT(S), MESSENGER(S), PAGE(S), and MAID(S); accordingly, we have not admitted these figures to the index. If, however, any of these character types has a proper name, we do, of course, index that name. Also, if any character is a specific type within the broad classification, we include him. For example, while we exclude SERVANT(S) (the general classification), we do include specific kinds of servants like BUTLER(S), CHAMBERLAIN(S), and FOOTMEN; and, though MAID(S) are not entered, we do index CHAMBERMAID(S), KITCHENMAID(S), and MAID(S) OF HONOUR. Just as we omit SERVANT(S) from classification in the index, so too do we exclude the Latin tags so frequently used for these characters. Thus, we do not admit the ANCILLAE who have parts in, among other plays, Thomas Garter's *The Most Virtuous and Godly Susanna* (1569; Greg no. 76.5; STC 11632a), George Chapman's *The Gentleman Usher* (1602; Greg no. 226; STC 4978), and John Stephens' *Cynthia's Revenge* (1613; Greg no. 314; STC 23248); neither do we include the APPARITOR(S) in Middleton's *The Family of Love* (1602; Greg no. 263; STC 17879) and in Fletcher and Massinger's *The Spanish Curate* (1622; Greg no. 638; STC B1581). KING(S), QUEEN(S), DUKE(S), and other members of the nobility we have omitted unless those general titles are the only identifying names used. Shakespeare's Sir John Falstaff is not indexed as a KNIGHT, but a nameless

[13]W. A. Armstrong, "The Elizabethan Conception of the Tyrant," *RES*, 22(1946), 161–81.

[14]See Fredson Bowers, "The Audience and the Poisoners of Elizabethan Tragedy," *JEGP*, 36(1937), 491–504 and Thomas P. Harrison, "The Literary Background of Renaissance Poisons," *Texas Studies in English*, 27(1948), 35–67; Richard H. Peake, "The Stage Prostitute in English Dramatic Tradition from 1558–1625," Unpublished dissertation, University of Georgia, 1967; Elbert N. S. Thompson, *The Controversy Between the Puritans and the Stage* (New York: Henry Holt, 1903) and Aaron M. Myers, "Representation and Misrepresentation of the Puritan in Elizabethan Drama," Unpublished dissertation, University of Pennsylvania, 1931.

[15]Inga-Stina Ewbank, " 'Those Pretty Devices': A study of Masques in Plays," in *A Book of Masques in Honor of Allardyce Nicoll*, ed. T. J. B. Spencer (Cambridge: Cambridge University Press, 1967), pp. 407–48.

[16]We have chosen to index rulers of cities or countries and the abstract figure of the city or country under the name of the city or country itself. Thus, the Duke of Venice would be entered under VENICE, as would the abstract figure VENICE. The citizens of Venice, however, have a separate entry under VENETIAN(S). But, whenever we had relatively few entries for any given city, country, or for its citizens, we chose to have a single entry for both. Thus, we enter the citizens of PADUA along with PADUA as: PADUA/PADUAN(S).

[17]We include Jews (following Edward D. Coleman, *The Jew in English Drama: An Annotated Bibliography* [New York: New York Public Library and Ktav Publishing, 1968]) in Greg nos. 177, 217, 303, 306, and 664. D. L. Cardozo (*The Contemporary Jew in English Drama* [Amsterdam: H. J. Paris, 1925]) would disagree with all of these entries, and Edgar Rosenberg (*From Shylock to Svengali: Jewish Stereotypes in English Fiction* [Stanford: Stanford University Press, 1960]) would query Greg nos. 217, 303, and 334.

one would be.[18] All adjectival descriptions which are part of a character's identification are included only when the playwright describes the character in no other way. Thus, Oedipus is not entered as a BLIND MAN, but a nameless blind soldier would be. Though a modern editor would give the first names of LATIMER, CRANMER, and RIDLEY in his edition of Thomas Drue's *The Duchess of Suffolk* (1624; Greg no. 451; STC 7242), we leave them out since Drue does not use them in his text. Since only BRISEIS is named among the five ladies accompanying the five heroes in William Cartwright's *The Siege* (1638; Greg no. 703; STC C709), we can only include her in the index. In Thomas Heywood's *2 The Iron Age* (1612; Greg no. 468; STC 13340), DIOMED is referred to as the King of AETOLIA, so AETOLIA is duly indexed; but, in *1 The Iron Age* (1612; Greg no. 467; STC 13340), DIOMED's kingship of AETOLIA is of no consequence, is not dealt with in the text, and so is not listed in the index. Similarly, while it is obvious that MELOSILE and MADINA are Ianthe's maids in both parts of William Davenant's *The Siege of Rhodes*, they are named only in the first part (1656; Greg no. 763; STC D339), not in the second (1659; Greg no. 827; STC D342), and are thus indexed only for the first part.

A final set of dramatic roles deserves special mention because of the difficulty of determining whether or not they actually were intended to be taken by actors. In many pageants, entertainments, and masques, the texts are often of little help in enabling the reader to decide whether an actor takes the role of a character or whether that character is a statue or a painting on the set. In Ben Jonson's *Lovers Made Men* (1617; Greg no. 350; STC 14775), for instance, HUMANITY, CHEERFULNESS, and READINESS are not characters but are parts of the arch-triumphal, and in William Davenant's *Salmacida Spolia* (1640; Greg no. 571; STC 6306), REASON, INTELLECTUAL APPETITE, COUNSEL, RESOLUTION, INTELLECTUAL LIGHT, DOCTRINE, DISCIPLINE, FAME, SAFETY, RICHES, FORGETFULNESS OF INJURIES, COMMERCE, FELICITY, AFFECTION TO THE COUNTRY, PROSPEROUS SUCCESS, and INNOCENCE are all part of the scenery described before the work begins. In such instances, these "characters" we do not include. Frequently, descriptions of allegorical representations are so syntactically convoluted that it is nearly impossible to determine what is and what is not the kind of figure we index. The following description, for instance, is from Middleton's *The Triumphs of Honour and Virtue* (1622; Greg no. 383; STC 17900):

> Next beneath *Antiquitie,* sit *Authoritie,* plac'd betweene *Wisedom & Innocence,* holding a naked sword, a serpent wound about the blade thereof, two Doves standing upon the cross bar of the hilt, and two hands meeting at the pummel, intimating *Mercy* and *Justice,* accompanied with *Magistracie.* . . . (Sig. B4ᵛ)

Since the lines suggest that *Mercy* and *Justice* are symbolized by the doves and the sword, we do not index MERCY or JUSTICE for this play, but we do include ANTIQUITY, AUTHORITY, WISDOM, and INNOCENCE since all are represented by persons.

We have tried to be as comprehensive as possible in terms of cross-references in the index without, at the same time, becoming overly obvious. It does not seem essential to cross-reference ANTONY, ANTHONY, and ANTONIO, and the like, for example; nor have we deemed it necessary to cross-reference such names as AVARICE, GREED, and COVETOUSNESS or LECHERY, LUST, and SENSUALITY. THELEMA and AMIANTEROS in William Davenant's *The Temple of Love* (1635; Greg no. 497; STC

---

[18]Variations upon this rule pertain also to characters such as WIFE, HUSBAND, and BROTHER. These are the only names given to three characters in Nathan Field's *Amends for Ladies* (1611; Greg no. 356; STC 10851), and so we include them in the index. For the same reasons, we have had to include the MOTHER and FATHER of the bride in Thomas Nabbes' *The Bride* (1638; Greg no. 576; STC 18338).

14719), for instance, also have the names WILL and CHASTE LOVE in the text; all four names we list but do not cross-reference. Similarly, we do not cross-reference MERCURY and HERMES, JUPITER and JOVE, or SOL, APOLLO, and PHOEBUS, and the like, but if such names appear interchangeably in any given text, as they do in Aston Cokain's *Trappolin Creduto Principe* (1633; Greg no. 796; STC C4894), then all such names are entered into the index, but not cross-referenced. A thesaurus might prove useful to a reader not entirely familiar with allegorical abstractions and classical deities. When a playwright uses definite abstract or classical groups in his play, we have listed them under their group as well as individually. Thus, whenever the nine muses appear, we index them under MUSES as well as under their individual names. The same method obtains for other collective characters like the FATES, DESTINIES, and SEVEN LIBERAL ARTS.

Some difficulty arose when we came to the listing of names that are identical to character types, abstractions, or nationalities. A character named CUTPURSE is easily distinguished from the thieving CUTPURSE(S) by using parentheses for the profession, just as the name SMITH differs from the profession SMITH(S). For differences between names like WILL (the shortened form of WILLIAM) and WILL (the abstraction), we are obliged to say (PROPER NAME) after the appropriate entry. The same device we use to distinguish between the feminine name FLORENCE and the ruler of the Italian city.

We hope that the index will have a variety of uses far broader than the one that gave it birth. Perhaps a student of the literature of the English Renaissance might want to trace the development of the allegorical figure FAME as that figure appears in plays spanning a century and a half. Or, an historian might be interested in the English image of NORWAY as reflected by the stage NORWEGIAN. A social historian might want to discover Renaissance English views towards various occupations—be they tailors, carpenters, or barbers. A literary historian may discover a name in the drama of the period which might lead him to an undiscovered source or analogue for a work written in the eighteenth, nineteenth, or twentieth centuries. In any case, we trust that the use of our index should be relatively simple. If one is interested in CARPENTER(S), for example, he would go to our listing for that occupation and discover the following numbers, all derived from Greg's *Bibliography of English Printed Drama to the Restoration:* 74, 155, 170, 277, 382, 403, 475, 488, 547, 603, 614, 736, 772, 798, and 807. He would then key those numbers to our Finding List. In the Finding List, he would discover that 74 refers to *2 Promos and Cassandra,* written by George Whetstone; that the play was printed in 1578 (Greg date); that it was probably first acted in 1578 (Harbage-Schoenbaum date); and that its *Short-Title Catalogue* number is 25347. Charles W. Camp's book, *The Artisan in Elizabethan Literature,*[19] listed in the Bibliography, might prove useful in considering CARPENTER(S).

No one realizes more than we the shortcomings of this index. Though we have tried to avoid arbitrary inclusions and omissions, some undoubtedly remain. Each of us has read every play at least twice, but there are, we are sure, characters we have missed. We urge students of the drama to communicate our omissions to us.

The authors gratefully acknowledge permissions from the Council of the Bibliographical Society to use material contained in W. W. Greg's *Bibliography of the English Printed Drama to the Restoration* and from the University of Pennsylvania Press to use material contained in Alfred Harbage's *Annals of English Drama, 975–1700,* revised by Samuel Schoenbaum. Further acknowledgements must be made to the following libraries and to their staffs: the Duke University Library, the University of North Carolina Library, the Macalester College Library, the University of Minnesota Library, the College of Charleston Library, the University of South Carolina Library, the St. Lawrence University

---

[19]New York: Columbia University Press, 1924.

Library, and, above all, the Folger Shakespeare Library. For various grants we wish to thank the Research Triangle Foundation, the Research Council of the University of North Carolina, Macalester College, and St. Lawrence University. The following persons contributed substantially to the preparation of the index: Virginia Kirby-Smith Carruthers, David Robinson, Ann Speltz, Deborah Diehl, James Carter, Janice Glickstein, Leigh Ford, Roberta B. Langford, Robert C. Branton, Jr., and Andrea Feldmann.

Thomas L. Berger
St. Lawrence University
Canton, New York

William C. Bradford, Jr.
College of Charleston
Charleston, South Carolina

Section II
The Index

379, 405, 408, 430, 445, 446, 454, 471, 533, 534, 553, 585, 645, 659, 775, 777, 786, 803, 806, 819
AGA   130, 430
AGAMEMNON   28, 42, 279, 382, 467, 468, 485, 789
AGAPE   200
AGAR   300
AGATHA   689, 766
AGATHE   241
AGATHOCLES   694
AGE   5
AGELASTUS   420
AGEN   520
AGENOR   328, 534, 552, 663, 750, 751, 779, 797
AGENS   746
AGENT(S)   133, 241, 248, 402, 434, 491, 720
AGER   352
AGERINUS   554
AGILITY   57
AGLAIA (SEE GRACES)   100, 164, 181, 202, 269, 271, 346, 791
AGLAOSI   448
AGLAURA   541, 629
AGNITES   218
AGNOSTUS   449
AGREEABLE   40
AGRICOLA   602
AGRICULTURE   731, 732
AGRIPPA   108, 147, 401, 405, 553, 823
AGRIPPINA   45, 216, 240, 554
AGRIPYNE   162
AGROICUS   547, 633
AGROTICUS   633
AGRYPINIA   200
AGUECHEEK   396
AGURTES   461
AGYDAS   94
AHIMAAS   160
AIMWELL   477
AIR   202, 208, 237, 324, 366, 514, 767, 778
AIRY SPIRITS   237, 411, 497
AJAX   279, 467, 789
AKERCOCK   826
ALABEZ   804
ALADIN   130, 458
ALAHAM   489
ALAMODE   473

ALANZO   490
ALARBUS   117
ALARI   834
ALASTO   661
ALASTOR   501
ALAZON   547
ALBA   453, 490, 765
ALBANACT   136, 218
ALBANACTUS   453
ALBANIA/ALBANIAN(S)   94, 218, 241, 482
ALBANO   252
ALBANY   39, 89, 112, 136, 265, 482
ALBERDURE   169
ALBERT   274, 300, 321, 656
ALBERTO   182, 184, 185, 199, 472, 519, 668, 723, 772
ALBERTUS   169, 197, 564, 729
ALBIN   753
ALBINA   752
ALBINIUS   156
ALBINOVANUS   122
ALBINUS   261, 626, 709
ALBION   38, 407
ALBIPOLIS   453
ALBIUS   186
ALBO   352
ALBON   531
ALBOVINE   422
ALBUMAZAR   330
ALCADE   445, 446, 819
ALCARIO   221
ALCHEMIST(S)   105, 303, 348, 497, 821
ALCIBIADES   402
ALCIDES   313
ALCIDON   649
ALCIPPUS   443
ALCMENA   81, 317
ALCON   118, 227, 499
ALDANA   509
ALDEBRAND   811
ALDERMAN(MEN)   74, 119, 142, 175, 220, 247, 400, 445, 460, 510, 591, 687, 688, 700
ALDRED   552
ALE   426, 507
ALECTO (SEE FURIES)   39, 104, 569, 673
ALEMAN(MEN)   166, 474
ALENÇON   150, 246, 307, 399

ALEPPO   430, 780
ALERAN   834
ALERZO   582
ALETHEIA   496
ALEWIFE(WIVES)   67, 151, 381, 820
ALEXANDER   119, 165, 220, 224,
    256, 279, 298, 367, 382, 447, 476, 491,
    498, 518, 644, 729, 773
ALEXANDER THE GREAT   84, 92,
    150, 157, 196, 205, 223, 260, 365, 367,
    458
ALEXANDRA   131, 308, 382
ALEXANDRIA   146, 553
ALEXANDRINO   434
ALEXANDRO   88, 110, 221
ALEXAS   405
ALEXIO   538
ALEXIS   287, 548, 557, 600, 654, 695,
    741
ALFEO   629
ALFONSO   725
ALFRED   472
ALFRIDA   115
ALFRIDE   772
ALGAZIER(S)   638, 661
ALGIERS/ALGERIAN(S)   446
ALGRIPE   574
ALGUAZIER(S)   661
ALIBIUS   712
ALICANT   712
ALICE   35, 101, 107, 165, 187, 455,
    558, 609, 722
ALICIA   718
ALIENA   394
ALIMONY LADY(IES)   802
ALINDA   647, 658, 810
ALISA   439
ALISANDRA   508
ALISON   35
ALIZIA   300
ALKAHAM   744
ALKEN   618
ALL FOR MONEY   72
ALL PRATE   697
ALLAN   565
ALLEGRE   550
ALLEN   351
ALLENSO   182
ALLMOUTH   465
ALLOBROGE(S)   296
ALLUM   250

ALLURED   531
ALLWIT   433
ALLY   718, 722
ALLY-BEG   744
ALMADO   716
ALMAINE   121, 162, 545
ALMANAC   358, 456
ALMANAC MAKER(S)   544, 635
ALMANSOR   804
ALMANZO   730
ALMANZOR   730, 804
ALMEDA   95
ALMENA   545
ALMENO   545
ALMERIN   621
ALMIRA   760
ALMONA   545
ALMS DEEDS   18
ALOISIO   538
ALONSO   192, 390, 471, 498, 525,
    598, 640, 669, 707, 712, 758
ALONZO   490, 758
ALOPE   530
ALPHABET   613
ALPHEGE   305
ALPHONSINA   508
ALPHONSO   169, 226, 277, 305, 384,
    386, 440, 505, 519, 599, 658, 665, 669,
    670, 716, 725, 727, 742, 759, 763, 810,
    814, 827, 835
ALPHONSUS   120, 156, 729
ALSEMERO   712
ALSIMIRA   723
ALTAMONT   428
ALTEA   598
ALTESTO   684
ALTEZA   428
ALTHA   574
ALTHEA   39, 313, 501, 605
ALTOFRONTO   203
ALTOMARO   479
ALTOPHIL   624
ALUPIS   539
ALURED   740
ALVA   192, 220
ALVARADO   707
ALVAREZ   490, 661, 707, 717, 727
ALVARO   336, 684
ALVERO   777
ALVIDA   118
ALVINO   255

ALWORTH   473, 474
ALYFACE   46
AMADA   286
AMADE   409
AMADIN   802
AMADINE   151, 506
AMADORE   834
AMAGO   315
AMALASUNTA   280
AMAN   33
AMANDA   581
AMANDUS   569
AMARANTA   624, 638
AMARANTHE   738
AMARILLIS   183, 227, 287, 504, 548,
    629, 756
AMARILLO   835
AMASA   160
AMASIA   783, 811
AMASIA/AMASIAN(S)   95, 130, 447
AMASIUS   704
AMAZON(S) (*SEE* SOLDIERESS(ES))
    156, 170, 184, 235, 280, 362, 402, 468,
    492, 571, 583, 604, 656, 657, 671, 701
AMBASSADOR(S)   101, 110, 113,
    117, 127, 165, 169, 197, 203, 212, 213,
    220, 221, 224, 248, 256, 274, 275, 295,
    306, 327, 398, 399, 400, 405, 406, 409,
    418, 447, 458, 467, 470, 479, 482, 491,
    493, 496, 497, 520, 521, 541, 552, 554,
    556, 569, 575, 584, 586, 648, 651, 654,
    671, 684, 701, 703, 736, 758, 772, 792,
    811, 835
AMBASSADRESS(ES)   827
AMBIDEXTER   56, 68
AMBIGAMOR   783
AMBIGUITY   556
AMBITIO   24
AMBITION   33, 61, 89, 93, 96, 180,
    290, 349, 355, 680
AMBITIOSO   253
AMBLE   474
AMBLER   407, 456, 457
AMBODEXTER   476, 587
AMBOIS   246, 307
AMBREE   411
AMBROSE   256, 549, 722, 806
AMBROSIA   501
AMBROSIUS   815
AMBUSH   257
AMELUS   480

AMERICA/AMERICAN(S)   310,
    320, 324, 366, 487, 775, 803
AMERULA   106
AMETHUS   420
AMIANA   832
AMIANTEROS   497
AMIDEA   498
AMIE   618, 708, 718
AMIENS   394, 662
AMILCAR   314
AMINADAB   191, 214, 815
AMINTA   417, 557, 653, 656, 812
AMINTAS   97, 106, 227, 548, 745, 756
AMINTER   235
AMINTOR   357, 704
AMITY   835
AMMON   160
AMMONIUS   63
AMORET   287
AMORETTA   555
AMORETTO   225
AMOROSO   230
AMOROUS   304, 587, 746
AMOROUS COURTIER(S)   571
AMOROUS MEN AND WOMEN
    497
AMOROUS SERVANT(S)   517
AMORPHO   567
AMORPHUS   181
AMOUR   502
AMPEDO   162
AMPHIABEL   531
AMPHIALUS   557
AMPHIBION   407
AMPHIBIUS   414
AMPHILUCHE   488
AMPHILUS   722
AMPHION   289, 411, 453
AMPHITRIO   317
AMPHITRION   34
AMPHITRITA   218
AMPHITRITE   419, 437, 466, 835
AMPHOTEROS   556
AMPHRIDOTE   567
AMPHRISA   530
AMPHRISUS   528, 529
AMPLE   507
AMSTERDAM   303, 699, 709
AMURACK   156
AMURATH   109, 130, 458
AMWELL-HEAD   312

15

333, 414, 426, 430, 435, 440, 445, 456,
495, 531, 535, 547, 562, 568, 601, 606,
638, 679, 699, 718, 721, 782, 788, 809,
821
APRICOCK   222
APRICOT WOMAN(WOMEN)   762
APSIA   709
APULEIUS   504, 698
AQUA   366
AQUA VITAE MAN(MEN)   643
AQUARIUS   271, 367, 496, 595, 778
AQUILA   595
AQUINAS   752
AQUITAINE   123, 398, 751
ARABIA/ARABIAN(S)   69, 94, 146,
155, 308, 569, 730
ARABIA BRITANNICA   202, 208
ARAGON   151, 156, 168, 172, 212,
215, 306, 368, 389, 400, 588, 657, 716,
725
ARAMANTHUS   164
ARAMNES   813
ARANE   360
ARASPAS   131
ARATHUSA   363
ARATUS   537
ARBACES   360, 580
ARBASTO   545
ARBITER   410
ARBITRATOR(S)   605
ARBONA   33
ARC   399
ARCADIA/ARCADIAN(S)   146, 164,
178, 227, 294, 313, 325, 394, 459, 499,
504, 530, 557, 583, 611, 625, 629, 741,
745
ARCADIUS   572
ARCANES   648
ARCAS   492, 611, 689
ARCASTUS   156
ARCATHIA   231
ARCATHIUS   122
ARCH INFORMER(S)   496
ARCHAS   294, 647, 689
ARCHBISHOP(S)   114, 129, 142, 145,
148, 165, 167, 215, 275, 295, 302, 400,
451, 603, 694, 729, 835
ARCHELAUS   122, 382
ARCHER(S)   136, 370
ARCHIAS   694
ARCHIBALD   145

ARCHIDAMUS   397, 408, 671
ARCHIGALLO   229
ARCHIGENES   499
ARCHILLUS   415
ARCHIMAGUS   593
ARCHIPPUS   570
ARCHIS   127
ARCHITECTURE   452
ARCHY   407, 686
ARCHYLLIS   12
ARCITE   492
ARDEA   273
ARDELIA   536, 667
ARDELIO   461
ARDELLAN   628
ARDEN   107, 275, 394
AREO   796
ARETAS   626
ARETE   162, 181, 202, 208, 302
ARETHUSA   317, 363, 602
ARETINA   518
ARETINUS   424
ARETUS   420, 667
AREUSA   439
ARGALO   545
ARGALUS   557
ARGENT   784
ARGERD   127
ARGES   294, 317
ARGESTES   537
ARGIA   450
ARGIER   94, 95
ARGILO   832
ARGIVE(S)   450, 467, 468
ARGONAUT(S)   313
ARGOS   313, 480, 485, 487, 663
ARGUILE   510
ARGURION   181, 202, 295, 355
ARGUS   301, 528
ARIADAN   95
ARIADNE   500, 734, 819
ARIAS   525, 596
ARIASPES   541
ARIEL   390
ARIENA   151
ARIENE   570
ARIES   271, 367, 496, 500, 595, 778
ARIETUS   605
ARIMATHEA   579
ARIOLA   506
ARION   335, 411, 453, 466

ASMOROTH   115
ASNATH   119
ASORINO   188
ASOTUS   181, 408, 469, 547
ASPASIA   146
ASPATIA   357
ASPER   163
ASPERO   268
ASPICE   552
ASS(ES)   106, 173, 320, 454, 504
ASSARACHUS   136
ASSASSINO   501
ASSAYER(S)   295
ASSISTANCE   268
ASSISTANT(S)   559
ASSISTANTE(S)   638, 661
ASSUERUS   33
ASSURANCE   59
ASSYRIA/ASSYRIAN(S)   118, 131,
    149
ASTAROTH   254
ASTEROTH   646
ASTELLA   429
ASTIANAX   28, 467, 468
ASTIOCHE   504
ASTLEY   491
ASTOLFO   305, 435
ASTON   153
ASTOR   254
ASTORAX   637
ASTORETH   254, 646
ASTORIUS   659
ASTRAEA   100, 202, 207, 208, 290,
    349, 500, 595
ASTRAEA VIRGO   695
ASTRINGER   395
ASTROLOGER(S)   78, 149, 205, 274,
    303, 330, 389, 411, 424, 469, 480, 500,
    554, 565, 616, 788
ASTROLOGIA   353, 595
ASTROLOGY   202
ASTRONOMER(S)   105, 368, 450,
    716
ASTRONOMIA   353, 595
ASTRONOMY   202, 208, 290, 302,
    322, 421, 670, 731, 732
ASTUTIO   470
ASTUTTA   719
ASYLUM, MASTER OF   658, 712
ATALANTA   280, 294, 313, 362

ATE   83, 136, 280
ATEUKIN   149
ATHAMAS   39
ATHEIST(S)   293
ATHELSTANE   162
ATHELSTONE   818
ATHENAIS   459
ATHENIO   626
ATHENODORUS   232, 444
ATHENS/ATHENIAN(S)   84, 120,
    170, 294, 384, 402, 415, 416, 420, 450,
    469, 492, 553, 584, 670, 699, 770
ATHEOS   709
ATIS   209
ATKINS   688
ATKINSON   451
ATLANTA   280, 294, 313, 362
ATLAS   321, 496, 608
ATOSSA   570
ATREBAS   482
ATREUS   29, 313
ATRIDES   703
ATRIUS   482
ATROPOS   83, 162, 202, 294, 317,
    324, 341, 350, 487, 600, 614, 626, 670,
    822
ATTARUS   223
ATTENDANCE   56
ATTICUS   252, 362
ATTILIA   86
ATTILIO   705
ATTORNEY(IES) (*SEE* LAWYER(S))
    153, 456, 473, 589, 609, 673, 699, 722,
    817, 835
ATTORNEY GENERAL   690
ATYCHES   443
AUBENY   418
AUBREY   180, 565
AUDACITY   181, 346
AUDAX   90, 746
AUDITOR   285
AUDITUS   4, 202, 208, 239, 311, 335,
    496, 514
AUDLEY   140, 516
AUDREY   262, 394, 463, 617
AUFIDIUS   401
AUGOIS   510
AUGUR(S) (*SEE* PROPHET(S))
    105, 232, 381, 444, 548
AUGUSTA   424, 554, 690

AUGUSTUS   186, 382, 553, 729
AULICUS   602
AUMALE   274, 307
AUMERLE   141
AUMONT   274
AURA   241, 584
AUREA   317
AURELIA   203, 281, 296, 362, 456,
    462, 470, 473, 536, 568, 582, 654, 693,
    704, 715, 779, 781
AURELIO   297, 418, 481, 555, 575,
    601
AURELIUS   120, 815, 822
AURIA   555
AURISTELLA   582
AURORA   207, 313, 339, 527, 529,
    607, 776
AUSBURGHER(S)   250
AUSONIUS   774
AUSPICES   237
AUSTELLA   750, 751
AUSTRACIA   368
AUSTRIA/AUSTRIAN(S)   101, 180,
    274, 398, 438
AUTEM-MORT   708
AUTHOR(S)   186, 481
AUTHORITY   70, 335, 383
AUTOLYCUS   397, 461
AUTRONIUS   296
AUTUMN   173, 313, 366, 376, 419,
    503, 529, 566, 767
AUVERGNE   274, 275, 399
AVARICE   17, 18, 25, 30, 59, 78, 182,
    205, 237, 325, 349
AVARITIA   24
AVARITIO   700
AVEIRO   220
AVERO   127, 220, 717
AVERY   679
AVOCATOR(I)   259
AVOLOS   478
AWDREY   262, 394, 463, 617
AYMER   464
AYRE   153, 154, 291, 332, 520
AZEVIDA   717
B   1, 2
BAB   586
BABIE-CAKE   606
BABILAS   715
BABOON(S)   309, 310, 492, 526, 787

BABULO   198
BABUS   308
BABYLON/BABYLONIAN(S)   95,
    156, 162, 241, 333, 818
BACCHA   328, 601
BACCHANALIAN(S)   767
BACCHANALL(S)   578
BACCHANTI   734
BACCHUS   83, 106, 124, 173, 186,
    239, 290, 366, 487, 543, 586, 734, 828
BACHA   328, 601
BACHELOR(S)   75, 194
BACKWINTER   173
BACON   121
BACTRIAN(S)   333
BACURIUS   360
BAD ANGEL(S)   205
BAD DAYS   358
BAD GENIUS   514, 760
BAGLIONE   478
BAGLIONI   254
BAGOA   99
BAGOLA   833
BAGOT   141, 189
BAGPIPER(S)   517, 543
BAG-SHOT   702
BAILIFF(S)   31, 67, 115, 166, 219,
    220, 464, 571, 602, 618, 669, 766
BAILO   61
BAILY   67, 76.5, 740
BAILY ERRAND   31
BAJAZET   94, 130, 156, 162, 458
BAJAZET II   447
BAKAM   650
BAKER(S)   455
BALANCE   323
BALBIANO   254
BALBUS   667
BALDOCK   129
BALDWIN   95, 565
BALE   22, 23, 24
BALIA   60, 206
BALIGNOSA   771
BALIGNY   307
BALL   114, 137, 510, 617
BALLAD MAN(MEN)   799, 836
BALLAD MONGER(S)   397
BALLAD SELLER(S)   93
BALLAD SINGER(S)   290, 455, 526,
    653, 803

BALLAD WOMAN(WOMEN)   586
BALLADING LOVER(S)   437
BALLADINO   281
BALLANCE   323
BALLIO   469
BALLIOL   112, 205
BALSARO   336
BALSERA   95
BALTAZAR   490, 777
BALTAZARO   562
BALTHASAR   143, 172
BALTHAZAR   110, 143, 168, 172,
    184, 185, 221, 281, 393, 490, 562, 707,
    777, 832
BALURDO   184, 185
BALWIN   565
BANAUSUS   547
BANBURY   455
BAND   326, 332, 456
BANDETTI (SEE HIGHWAYMAN
    (MEN))   333, 402, 434, 446, 486
    582, 689, 724, 759, 792
BANDINO   254
BANDWINE   835
·BANELASS   806
BANESWRIGHT   568
BANISTER   126, 189
BANKS   264, 785
BANKSIDE   259, 455
BANQUO   404
BANTAM   494
BAPTIST(S)   22, 623
BAPTISTA   120, 188, 197, 388, 436,
    508, 668
BAPTISTO   545
BARABAS   475
BARBARA   586, 632, 692
BARBARIAN(S)   351, 454
BARBARINO   796
BARBARISM   311
BARBAROSO   316
BARBAROSSA   162, 254
BARBARY   94, 156, 224, 471, 777
BARBAZELLA   626
BARBER(S)   63, 106, 112, .214, 254,
    262, 297, 304, 316, 320, 382, 456, 464,
    490, 501, 518, 532, 558, 577, 580, 602,
    702, 757, 785, 807, 815, 821
BARBERY   492
BARCELES   127
BARCELONA   471, 669

BARD(S)   327, 347, 355, 482, 593, 791
BARDH   327
BARDOLPH   145, 165, 167, 187
BAREBOTTLE   693
BARGEMAN(MEN)   114
BARIO   206
BARKER   549
BARLEY   158
BARMONDSAY   302
BARNABAS   31
BARNABE   171, 442, 531
BARNABY   507
BARNACLE   523
BARNADINE   392
BARNARD   242
BARNARDINE   475
BARNARDO   197, 254
BARNE   771, 796
BARNES   155, 161
BARNET   442, 484, 784
BARNHAM   673
BARON(S)   112, 366
BARONIA   434
BARREL(S)   608
BARREN   510
BARRISOR   246
BARSENE   671
BARTELLO   664
BARTERVILE   305
BARTHOLOMEUS   835
BARTHOLOMEW   120, 323, 442, 455
BARTLEY   249
BARTOLUS   638
BARTRAM   149
BARTUS   133
BARWICK   215, 510
BARYTE   269
BASE   652
BASE PORT   835
BASHAW(S)   94, 110, 127, 130, 248,
    278, 430, 445, 446, 447, 458, 475, 489,
    622, 763, 780, 793, 827
BASHFUL SCHOLAR(S)   547
BASHFULNESS   434
BASILINO   797
BASILISCO   109
BASILIUS   43, 235, 583
BASILONTE   832
BASKET   617
BASKET MAKER(S)   198, 586, 836
BASKET MAN(MEN)   323

22

BELCHAR 254

BELCHER 205

BELDAM(S) 294

BELERRIO 791

BELFARE 425

BELFOREST 293

BELFRIDA 626

BELGARDE 559

BELGIAN PROVINCES 202, 208

BELGIOSA 418

BELGIUM/BELGIAN(S) 482

BELIALO 434

BELIARBY 278

BELIERBEY 130

BEL-IMPERIA 110, 221

BELINDA 429, 695, 738

BELINUS 156, 482

BELIZA 663

BELLA FRANCA 333

BELLAFLORA 773

BELLAFRONT 204, 299, 435

BELLAMENTE 573

BELLAMIA 521

BELLAMIE 540, 592, 718

BELLAMINO 811

BELLAMIRA 210, 475

BELLAMONT 250

BELLAMORE 563

BELLAMOUR 518

BELLAMY 592, 718

BELLANIMA 514

BELLANORA 219

BELLAPERT 464

BELLARIO 363, 690

BELLARMINE 586

BELLARMINO 434

BELLARMO 690

BELLAURA 747

BELLEROPHON 317, 526

BELLERRIO 791

BELLESA 797

BELLEUR 706

BELLICOSUS 704

BELLIDES 653

BELLIÈVRE 274, 275

BELLINA 533

BELLINDA 429, 695, 738

BELLINGHAM 632

BELLIRA 704

BELLIZARIUS 533

BELLMAN(MEN) 214, 336, 388, 389, 527, 574, 776

BELLONA 365, 419, 453, 522, 626

BELLOWS MENDER(S) 170, 611

BELLULA 290, 539

BELLUTUS 401

BELMONT 172

BELOVED NOT LOVING 16

BELOVED PEOPLE 571

BELPHEGOR 673.5, 826

BELSISE 617

BELT 808

BELTAZAR 744

BELVIDERE 664

BENATZI 555

BENEDICK 168, 264

BENEDICT 204

BENEDICTINE(S) 429, 815

BENEFIAN 744

BENEVEMUS 226

BENEVENTI 581

BENHADAD 802

BENINGFIELD 215

BENJAMIN 337, 710

BENNETT 242

BENNINGTON 215

BENTHUSIN 643

BENTIVOGLIO 599

BENTIVOLI 254

BENTIVOLIO 188, 536

BENVOGLIO 670

BENVOLIO 143, 205

BENWASH 300

BERALDO 435

BERECYNTHIA 137

BERENICE 280

BERENICES 595

BERGER 159

BERGETTO 486

BERINTHIA 562

BERKELEY 129, 141, 142

BERMUDO 685

BERNARD 364, 561

BERNARDIA 835

BERNARDO 197, 254, 423, 505, 747, 779

BEROE 269, 317

BERONTE 649

BERONTES 313

BEROSUS 626

BRISK 163
BRISKIE 647
BRISSAC 714
BRISSONET 657
BRISTLE 455, 799
BRISTOL 129, 448, 700
BRISTOW 66, 211
BRITAEL 482
BRITAIN (*SEE* BRITON(S)) 39, 89,
    101, 102, 136, 213, 233, 265, 288, 327,
    342, 355, 398, 406, 482, 496, 527, 531,
    571, 815, 822
BRITANIA 803
BRITANIDES 527
BRITANNICA 200, 202, 208
BRITANNICUS 554
BRITANOCLES 526
BRITOMART 512
BRITON(S) 380, 482, 512, 551, 552,
    574, 593, 655, 815
BRITTANIA 218, 419
BRITTANY/BRETON(S) 89
BRITTLE JOY 104
BRITTLEWARE 587
BROCKET 215
BROKENBERY 126, 142, 154
BROKER(S) 70, 115, 189, 236, 266,
    389, 456, 457, 508, 568, 602, 825
BROMIUS 548
BROMLEY 337
BRONTES 271, 421, 614
BROOK 187
BROOKEALL 722
BROOKS 773
BROOM MAID(S) 226
BROOM MAN(MEN) 226, 799
BROOM SELLER(S) 85, 647
BROOME 187
BROTES 660
BROTHEL 276
BROTHER(S) 356, 524, 652
BROUGHTON 179
BROWNE 155, 212, 224, 336, 383,
    673, 686
BROWNIST(S) 829
BROWSILDORA 588
BRUCE 112, 180, 520, 749
BRUGES 643
BRUINE 460
BRULART 274

BRUN 180, 699
BRUNDUSIUS 605
BRUNEL 275
BRUNETTO 796
BRUNHALT 368
BRUNO 74, 205
BRUNSWICK 169, 451
BRUSCO 624
BRUSH MAN(MEN) 799
BRUSOR 109
BRUTE 218
BRUTUS 116, 122, 136, 232, 261,
    273, 401, 403, 444
BRUZANTIA 791
BRYAN 157, 435, 507
BUBBLE 323
BUBBLE(S) 711
BUBIE 565
BUBO 195
BUBULCUS 441
BUCEPHALUS 717
BUCHANAN 487
BUCKCLOUG 585
BUCKINGHAM 119, 126, 142, 154,
    302, 400, 491, 585
BUCKLER MAKER(S) 220
BUCOLIAN 232
BUD 762
BUDA 95
BUDGE 825
BUDGET 589, 799
BUFFETER(S) 453
BUFFONE 163, 792
BUFO 314, 716
BUGARGO 791
BUGGE 226
BUILDER(S) 808
BULFINCH 463
BULFLESH 796
BULGARIA/BULGARIAN(S) 458
BULL(S) 313, 686, 816
BULLAKER 228
BULLCALF 167
BULLEN 400
BULLIS 806
BULLITHRUMBLE 130
BULLOIN 332
BULLY 465
BUM 392
BUMBLE 831

BUMM   507
BUMP   722
BUMPKIN   754
BUMPKIN(S)   779
BUMPSEY   722
BUNCH   171
BUNDRUCIA   280
BUNDUCA   280
BUNG   799
BUNGAY   121
BUNGHOLE   748
BUNGLER   266
BUONATESTE   506
BURBAGE   203, 225
BURBIANO   418
BURDEN   121
BURGARGO   791
BURGES   686
BURGESS(ES)   194, 225, 803
BURGH   101, 102, 180, 182, 398
BURGHER(S)   63, 122, 192
BURGIO   719
BURGOMASTER(S)   146, 451, 643
BURGONIA   750, 751
BURGUNDY/BURGUNDIAN(S)
        148, 154, 165, 171, 265, 399, 641
BURLAMEO   689
BURLEIGH   673
BURNED CHILD(CHILDREN)   410
BURNING PESTLE   316
BURNISH   214
BURNOMOY   791
BURRATINE(S)   607
BURRHUS   554
BURRIS   647
BURST   442
BURY   180
BUSHELL   511
BUSHY   141
BUSINESS   18, 613
BUSK   220
BUSSY   246, 307
BUSTOFA   653
BUSY   455, 476, 591
BUSYRIS   313
BUTAS   444
BUTCHER(S)   41, 119, 155, 217, 225,
        407, 503, 671, 709, 796, 799, 806
BUTLER   249, 564
BUTLER(S)   161, 166, 258, 292, 303,

308, 390, 429, 465, 515, 565, 617, 660,
        693, 708, 766
BUTTER WOMAN(WOMEN)   456
BUTTERICKE   336
BUTTON MAKER(S)   815
BUTTS   400
BUZ   407, 456
BUZARAIN   791
BUZARDO   508
BUZZARD   806
BYDE   688
BYDETT   252
BYLLIUS   147
BYPLAY   586
BYRON   95, 274, 275
BYRRIA   12, 91, 415
BYTHEAS   231
BYTHINIA/BYTHINIAN(S)   513,
        671
BYZANGES   550
BYZANTIUM/BYZANTINE(S)   703,
        745
CABLE   831
CABRADO   362
CACAFOGO   598
CACONOS   78
CADALLAN   327
CADDY(IES)   278
CADE   119, 526
CADIZ   220
CADOR   89, 822
CADUSIA/CADUSIAN(S)   541
CADWALL   406
CAELESTINE   195
CAELICA   489
CAELIO   277, 728, 742
CAENIS   424
CAESAR   92, 108, 116, 122, 127, 132,
        147, 186, 216, 232, 261, 283, 296, 327,
        365, 367, 380, 382, 403, 405, 410, 424,
        444, 453, 482, 531, 553, 554, 578, 645,
        654, 667, 698, 823
CAESARE   254
CAESARIA/CAESARIAN(S)   380
CAESARIO   132, 396, 519, 668
CAFFARES   771
CAIAPHAS   579
CAIAZZO   418
CAIGUBUS   447
CAIN   155

CARICLEA 584
CARICLES 584
CARILLUS 620
CARINNA 122
CARINO 183, 629
CARINTHA 545, 577
CARINTHIA 545
CARINUS 12, 91, 156, 227
CARIO 759
CARIOLA 389
CARION 60, 699, 805
CARIONIL 771
CARISOPHUS 58
CARLILE 409
CARLISLE 141
CARLO 163, 253, 305, 306, 418, 479, 490, 728, 774, 792
CARLOS 723, 814
CARMAN(MEN) 580, 586
CARMONIA/CARMONIAN(S) 95
CARNAL CONCUPISCENCE 47
CARNUTIUS 698
CAROL 606
CAROLA 626
CAROLL 517
CAROLO 300, 305, 435, 505, 742
CAROLUS 364, 729
CARONNIO 811
CAROPIA 730
CARPENTER(S) 74, 155, 170, 277, 382, 403, 475, 488, 547, 603, 614, 736, 772, 798, 807
CARRACK 831
CARRACUS 321
CARRADIN 458
CARRICK 520
CARRIER(S) (SEE PORTER(S)) 145, 148, 166, 274, 316
CARROL 445
CARTANDES 552
CARTASMANDA 327
CARTER 114, 785
CARTER(S) 162, 205, 258, 397, 729, 801, 823
CARTERTON 542
CARTESMUNDA 740
CARTHAGE/CARTHAGINIAN(S) 128, 231, 513, 533
CARTHAGINIAS 128
CARTHALON 231
CARTHUSIAN(S) 624

CARTISMANDA 327
CARTOPHYLAX 246
CARVEGUT 476
CARVER(S) 614, 835
CARVILIUS 482
CASBERT 673
CASBIN 248
CASCA 232, 403
CASH 176, 809
CASHIER(S) 176, 220, 257
CASIMIR 224
CASPILONA 626
CASSANA 654
CASSANDER 260, 572
CASSANDRA 42, 73, 74, 279, 467, 468, 485, 519, 665
CASSIANO 479
CASSIBELANE 482
CASSIBELLANUS 482
CASSILANE 648
CASSIMERE 169
CASSIMERO 221
CASSIMIRUS 729
CASSIO 314, 379, 599
CASSIOPEIA 466, 500, 595
CASSIUS 116, 232, 261, 296, 403
CASTA 670
CASTABELLA 293, 562
CASTADORA 741
CASTALIA 557
CASTAMELLA 532
CASTANNA 555
CASTARINA 761
CASTEL-BLANCO 669
CASTELLANO(ES) 728
CASTER 702, 762
CASTIBULA 90
CASTIGATIO 202
CASTILE 110, 112, 121, 221, 398, 440, 525, 588, 596, 729
CASTILIAN(S) 162, 184, 254, 388, 440, 491, 525, 588, 596, 670, 826
CASTILIANO 826
CASTILIO 184, 185
CASTILLA 717
CASTINA 241
CASTIZA 243, 253, 815
CASTOR 313, 332, 467, 803
CASTRAGANIO 506, 833
CASTRATO 714
CASTRE 706

257, 264, 361, 398, 400, 442, 485, 491,
585, 649, 689, 713, 773, 835
CHAMBERMAID(S)   99, 258, 292,
396, 441, 442, 456, 469, 474, 476, 477,
514, 535, 594, 690, 692, 702, 703, 720,
729
CHAMBERS   211
CHAMBRENSIS   605
CHAMLET   587, 821
CHAMONT   281, 559
CHAMP   406
CHAMPAIGNE   192
CHAMPERNELL   639
CHAMPERTY   290
CHAMPION(S)   86, 100, 129, 237,
327, 332, 333, 428, 457, 467, 823, 835
CHAMPIONS OF CHRISTENDOM
545
CHAMUS   443
CHANCELLOR(S)   63, 215, 249, 275,
302, 306, 400, 451, 550, 565, 725, 729,
835
CHANDLER(S)   153, 182, 293, 328
CHANDOS   215
CHANGEABLE   561
CHANGECOAT   321
CHANGELING(S)   712, 806
CHANGELOVE   540
CHANON   617
CHAOS-AP-DEMOGORGON-AP-
ETERNITY   496
CHAPLAIN(S) (*SEE* PRIEST(S))
63, 138, 293, 451, 474, 491, 556, 618,
708, 784
CHAPMAN(MEN)   153, 460
CHARALOIS   464
CHARASTUS   685
CHARIFA   804
CHARILLA   572
CHARILUS   469
CHARINO   640
CHARINTHA   428, 599
CHARINTHUS   651
CHARINUS   12, 91, 325, 415, 499,
654
CHARIOLUS   602
CHARIOTEER(S)   488
CHARISSA   720
CHARISTUS   701
CHARITA   737

CHARITIES   164, 202, 271
CHARITY   18, 20, 30, 40, 72, 100,
387, 409, 434, 448, 483, 546, 786
CHARLATAN(S)   705
CHARLEMAGNE   365
CHARLES   112, 212, 258, 274, 275,
316, 333, 365, 394, 399, 438, 515, 585,
680, 714
CHARLES I OF ENGLAND   496,
585, 677, 680
CHARLES I OF FRANCE   365
CHARLES V OF FRANCE   400
CHARLES V OF GERMANY   212,
386
CHARLES VI OF FRANCE   148, 165
CHARLES VII OF FRANCE   399
CHARLES VIII OF FRANCE   254
CHARLES IX OF FRANCE   133
CHARLES OF BURGUNDY   154
CHARLES OF GERMANY   205, 212
CHARLES OF NORMANDY   140
CHARLMONT   293
CHARLOTTE   246, 307, 639, 662
CHARM   434
CHARMI   464
CHARMIA   742
CHARMIO   553
CHARMION   108, 132, 405
CHARNEL   158
CHAROMONTE   505
CHARON   124, 221, 305, 350, 504,
637, 788
CHARTHAM   119
CHARTLEY   250, 535
CHARTRES   166, 275
CHARWOMAN(WOMEN)   442, 526
CHARYLUS   469
CHASE ILLIBEGGE   458
CHASTE LOVE   497
CHASTITY   18, 76, 124, 155, 193,
194, 275, 311, 409, 466, 670, 823
CHAT   67
CHATILLON   307, 398
CHATTILION   101
CHAUCER   349, 409
CHAUGH   352
CHAVES   707
CHAWGH   352
CHEATER(S)   266, 442, 460, 565,
702, 773, 792, 801, 815

CHURCHWARDEN(S)   137, 547
CHURFURST(S)   729
CHURL(S)   72, 83
CHURMS   234
CIBILE   584
CICELY   442, 540
CICERO   116, 232, 261, 283, 296, 403,
    698
CICILIA   444, 540, 619, 828
CID   525, 596
CILICIA/CILICIAN(S)   118, 444, 567
CILIUS   828
CILLARUS   317
CIMBER   296, 403
CIMBRIO   408
CIMENA   525, 596
CINEDO   163
CINGETORIX   482
CINNA   122, 403
CINQUE-PORTS   174, 400
CINXIA   237
CIPRES   729
CIRCE   443, 454
CIRCULARITY   269
CIRCUMSPECTION   11, 202, 208
CIRCUMSPICE   522
CIS   690
CITHERIA   504, 627
CITIZEN(S)   52, 64, 68, 74, 84, 85, 93,
    94, 95, 101, 110, 113, 119, 120, 122, 126,
    135, 140, 142, 143, 153, 155, 158, 165,
    170, 171, 175, 179, 189, 192, 204, 206,
    217, 220, 222, 244, 245, 248, 251, 257,
    259, 276, 277, 283, 284, 285, 290, 292,
    298, 299, 316, 320, 323, 328, 330, 333,
    347, 353, 356, 360, 363, 388, 392, 395,
    398, 400, 401, 403, 415, 416, 425, 426,
    435, 438, 440, 442, 444, 451, 460, 465,
    468, 470, 472, 473, 481, 484, 486, 489,
    523, 535, 537, 540, 553, 555, 565, 568,
    570, 576, 579, 584, 586, 591, 601, 605,
    626, 628, 630, 632, 650, 651, 657, 658,
    660, 662, 665, 669, 671, 672, 689, 694,
    697, 700, 702, 703, 711, 715, 718, 721,
    724, 725, 746, 749, 750, 760, 761, 762,
    773, 774, 777, 782, 783, 788, 792, 793,
    802, 803, 806, 808, 809, 810, 815, 821,
    823, 824
CITWIT   720
CITY   366
CITY WELL GOVERNED   448

CIVET   222
CIVIL GOVERNMENT   412
CLACK   708, 826
CLAIUS   548
CLAMYDES   157
ÇLARA   456, 597, 598, 661, 717, 728
CLARAMANTE   832
CLARAMONT   156
CLARANGE   649
CLARATHEA   709
CLARE   102, 112, 129, 249, 257, 264,
    388, 477, 591, 817
CLARELLA   532
CLARENCE   126, 138, 142, 154, 165,
    167, 228, 302
CLARENTIA   215
CLARIANA   539, 573
CLARIBELL   362
CLARICILLA   620
CLARIDIANA   315
CLARIFLORA   580
CLARIMANT   750, 751
CLARIMOND   737
CLARIMONT   811
CLARINA   814
CLARINDA   423, 470, 649, 656, 698,
    742
CLARINDO   325
CLARINGTON   785
CLARION   618
CLARISIA   69
CLARISSA   668
CLARISSIMO   259, 297
CLARKE   107
CLARO   717
CLAUDIA   600, 667
CLAUDIANA   747
CLAUDIO   168, 219, 392, 403, 664,
    726, 759
CLAUDIUS   65, 197, 240, 327, 403,
    554, 578, 605, 733
CLAUSE   643
CLAVEELE   471
CLAY   617
CLEAGENOR   790
CLEANDER   60, 499, 537, 649, 694,
    751
CLEANLINESS   47
CLEANTES   551, 552
CLEANTHA   588
CLEANTHE   637, 771

COMMANDER(S)   222, 265, 279,
    387, 410, 420, 525, 533, 554, 588, 602,
    619, 626, 655, 659, 668, 680, 685, 694,
    698, 733, 774, 776, 828
COMMERCE   383, 800
COMMING   520
COMMISERATION   351
COMMISSARY   680, 835
COMMISSIONER(S)   274, 520
COMMITTEE-MAN(MEN)   605,
    630, 679, 709
COMMON   303
COMMON CONDITIONS   69
COMMON COUNSEL   678.5
COMMON CURSE   630, 631
COMMON PLEAS   835
COMMON THEFT   194
COMMON THRIFT   194
COMMONER(S)   52, 401, 403
COMMONS   48
COMMONS' COMPLAINT   56
COMMONS' CRY   56
COMMONWEAL   194
COMMONWEALTH   75, 96
COMMUNIS SENSUS   239
COMO   241
COMODUS   690
COMOLET   246
COMPANIES OF LONDON   302,
    332, 466
COMPANION(S)   481
COMPASS   616, 817
COMPASSION   434
COMPLAINT   56
COMPLEMENT   414
COMPLEMENTER(S)   720
COMPLEXIONS (*SEE* HUMOURS)
    514, 767
COMPLICE(S)   702
COMPOSER(S)   802
COMPOSITOR(S)   385
COMPTON   212
COMPTROLLER(S)   835
COMUS   374, 524, 608
COMYN   520
CONALLUS   593
CONAN   89
CONCEIT   11, 547, 767
CONCHYLIO   443
CONCLAVIST(S)   306
CONCLUSION   556

CONCORD   96, 144, 233, 453, 496,
    571, 670
CONCORDIA   207
CONCUBINE(S)   95, 160, 166, 223,
    424, 428, 458, 472, 554, 744, 810
CONCUPISCENCE   47, 688, 746
CONDÉ   133
CONDELL   203
CONDITIONS   69
CONFECTIONER(S)   549, 776
CONFESSION   4
CONFESSOR(S)   246, 362, 388, 412,
    430, 470, 486, 603, 702, 723, 749, 815,
    816
CONFIDANT(S)   429, 518, 553, 573,
    588, 620, 621, 622, 701, 721, 725, 727,
    738, 759, 771, 802
CONFIDENCE   434, 488
CONFIDENT   521
CONFUSION   53
CONFUSION AND HORROR OF MIND
    78
CONJUROR(S) (*SEE* MAGICIAN(S))
    119, 121, 137, 205, 241, 246, 251, 264,
    306, 353, 393, 431, 462, 646, 796
CONJURESS(ES)   313
CONON   663
CONQUEST   89, 473
CONRADE   168, 422
CONSCIENCE   5, 30, 65, 78, 85, 93,
    335, 367, 383, 514
CONSOLARIO   569
CONSOLATION   49
CONSORT(S)   802
CONSPICE   522
CONSPIRACY   635
CONSPIRATOR(S)   166, 306, 401,
    403, 410, 424, 537, 541
CONSTABARUS   308
CONSTABLE(S)   14, 58, 85, 99, 111,
    121, 148, 150, 154, 163, 165, 168, 174,
    182, 188, 190, 211, 212, 214, 215, 217,
    229, 237, 243, 266, 276, 283, 290, 292,
    337, 384, 392, 400, 435, 451, 457, 461,
    463, 475, 476, 488, 490, 491, 494, 501,
    507, 533, 542, 550, 561, 574, 580, 586,
    591, 592, 615, 617, 626, 628, 631, 632,
    644, 653, 661, 666, 692, 697, 702, 708,
    717, 762, 772, 773, 776, 785, 788, 802,
    810, 824, 825, 829, 835
CONSTANCE   101, 180, 398, 463

(MEN))   39, 89, 115, 129, 162,
175, 213, 265, 289, 327, 482, 615, 729,
822
CORNWELL   229
COROMBONA   306
CORONA   500
CORONA BOREA   595
CORPORAL(S)   165, 167, 204, 251,
516, 655, 659, 670, 709, 740, 828
CORRASO   361
CORRECTION   70, 193, 194, 247
CORRECTOR(S)   225
CORRODINO   139
CORRUPT LOVER(S)   437
CORRUPT REASON   489
CORRUPTION   349
CORSA   427
CORSICA/CORSICAN(S)   555
CORSITES   99
CORTES   717, 752
CORTEZZA   226
CORTICEUS   605
CORVINO   259, 581
CORVINUS   74
CORYBREUS   593
CORYMBUS   548
CORYN   106, 157, 394
COS   181
COSIMO   427, 505
COSMA   443
COSMETA   701
COSMO   498, 501, 533, 736, 741
COSROE   94, 654
COSSIN   133
COSTARD   150
COSTERMONGER(S)   148, 162, 455,
606
COSTIN   643
COT-QUEEN(S)   836
COTSHOLDE   111
COTSWOLD   322
COTTA   216
COTTER(S)   193
COTUS   401
COUCHBACK   112
COULTER   587
COUNSEL   26, 41, 47, 48, 56, 193,
200, 202, 208, 322, 335, 355, 635.5, 678.5
COUNSELLOR(S) (*SEE* STATES-
MAN(MEN)   17, 18, 39, 56, 58,

74, 88, 89, 106, 109, 142, 146, 151, 165,
167, 184, 197, 209, 223, 239, 241, 248,
267, 278, 308, 357, 362, 384, 386, 390,
392, 420, 424, 434, 436, 450, 453, 458,
470, 472, 480, 481, 482, 491, 493, 499,
505, 513, 518, 531, 538, 541, 547, 551,
552, 553, 554, 556, 559, 565, 570, 578,
582, 604, 618, 621, 645, 647, 664, 665,
671, 684, 690, 694, 703, 716, 730, 735,
744, 746, 749, 772, 780, 807, 810, 813,
817, 835
COUNTERBUFF   821
COUNTERFEIT COUNTE   11
COUNTRY   87, 366
COUNTRY BOOR(S)   802
COUNTRY BRIDE(S)   613
COUNTRY CLOWN(S)   309, 758
COUNTRY DANCER(S)   524
COUNTRY FELLOW(S)   56, 258,
363, 394, 441, 488, 512, 547, 580, 587,
694, 702, 767
COUNTRY GENTLEMAN(MEN)
124, 204, 276, 277, 321, 354, 364, 416,
427, 507, 515, 523, 540, 542, 571, 586,
632, 641, 644, 659, 720, 761, 788, 808,
821
COUNTRY GENTLEWOMAN
(WOMEN)   245, 276, 277
COUNTRY GIRL(S)   632
COUNTRY GULL(S)   176
COUNTRY JUSTICE(S)   167, 187,
615
COUNTRY KNIGHT(S)   477, 591,
831
COUNTRY LASS(ES)   494
COUNTRY MAID(S)   256, 318, 653,
826
COUNTRY MUSICIAN(S)   98
COUNTRY PLAYER(S)   815
COUNTRY REAPER(S)   390
COUNTRY SERVANT(S)   722
COUNTRY SOLDIER(S)   167
COUNTRY SQUIRE(S)   121
COUNTRY SWAIN(S)   496, 545,
699, 803
COUNTRY TAILOR(S)   705
COUNTRY WENCH(ES)   121, 150,
258, 309, 317, 394, 433, 493, 504, 632,
754, 767
COUNTRYMAN(MEN) (*SEE*

DE TOLEDO   729
DE TORMES   188
DE TOTTENHAM   835
DETRACTIO   202
DETRACTION   202, 208, 362, 691,
   767
DE TRIPES   729
DE VALDES   224
DE VARANA   532
DE VENTURO   446
DE VERMINI   661
DEVICE   681
DEVIL(S) (*SEE* DEMON(S))   41, 50,
   54, 64, 72, 76.5, 78, 115, 118, 121, 124,
   205, 246, 251, 254, 264, 276, 278, 290,
   299, 305, 317, 365, 444, 452, 457, 497,
   501, 514, 527, 545, 558, 561, 593, 628,
   646, 654, 672, 673.5, 697, 700, 772, 785,
   792, 796, 822, 826
DE VILAREZO   562
DE VILE   490
DE VITELLI   661
DE VITRY   368
DEVONSHIRE   222, 815
DEVOTION   57, 93, 193, 448
D'HAUVRYE   192
DIACONATUS   63
DIAGORUS   357
DIANA   75, 83, 90, 105, 124, 171, 207,
   284, 294, 385, 395, 453, 458, 537, 549,
   586, 595, 670, 695, 754, 790
DIANETTA   774
DIAPHANE   269
DIAPHANOUS   616
DIAPHANTA   583, 712
DI ARCHAS   689, 735
DIAS   650
DIASTROPHE   434
DICACHE   195
DICAEARCHE   496
DICAEUS   443, 699
DICASTES   602
DICCON   67, 504
DICER   190
DICHE (*SEE* GRACES)   98, 202, 208,
   340, 488, 529, 627, 670
DICHU   593
DICK   15, 48, 68, 105, 107, 119, 149,
   161, 166, 190, 203, 205, 210, 222, 225,
   242, 244, 262, 276, 352, 433, 460, 585,
   693, 796, 825, 829

DICKISON   494
DICQUE   236
DIDIMO   519
DIDO   92, 128, 617
DIDYMUS   789
DIEGO   127, 525, 562, 596, 638, 669,
   717, 723, 832
DIFFICULT   244
DIGGON   83
DIGHTON   154
DIGNITAS   270
DIGNITY   269
DIGUE   236
DIJON   464
DILATOR GENERAL   496
DILDO   184
DILDOMAN   440
DILIGENCE   52, 55, 56, 85, 93, 155,
   193, 194, 495
DI MALFA   689
DI MATTALOON   689
DINANT   639
DING'EM   788
DINOMACHUS   701
DINON   131
DIOCLES   654
DIOCLESIAN   380, 531, 654
DIOCLESIANO   434
DIOGENES   84, 617, 770
DIOMEDE   108, 467, 468
DIOMEDES   132, 279, 405, 789
DION   363, 397, 619, 620
DIONYSIA   471, 806
DIONYSIO   536
DIONYSIUS   58, 455
DIONYZA   284
DIOPHANTES   738
DIPHILUS   357, 408
DI POPOLO   689
DIPSAS   99, 469, 633
DIPWELL   636
DIRCETUS   108, 132
DIRCUS   450
DIRECTORY   636
DIROT   113
DIRT   382
DISANIUS   807
DISCIPLE(S)   414, 461, 732
DISCIPLINE   53, 335
DISCOPIO   811
DISCORD   61, 83, 144, 232, 571, 586

DRYAD(ES) (*SEE* WOOD NYMPH(S))
   339, 362, 454, 731, 732
DRYFAT   263
DRYGROUND   722
DUARTE   427, 640
DUBOIS   662
DUBON   214
DU CHAMP   406
DUCHESS(ES)   253
DUCK(S)   290, 298
DU CROY   464
DUDGEON   153
DUDLEY   212, 256
DUELLONA   522
DUKE(S)   92, 253, 366, 412, 423
DULA   357
DULCIFLORA   580
DULCIMELL   230
DULCIMENTA   597
DULCINO   429
DULICHYA   789
DULYPO   60
DULESSE   291
DULIS   626
DULL   150, 704
DULL LOVER(S)   437
DULL-PATE   699
DUMAINE   133, 150, 395, 714
DUMB MEN/WOMEN   732, 810
DUNCAN   404
DUNGHILL RAKER(S)   748
DUNGO   836
DUNGWORTH   542
DUNMOW   180, 749
DUNS   487
DUNSTABLE   166
DUNSTAN   115, 295, 826
DU PONT   656
DU PRETTE   565
DURABLE   580
DURAZZO   759
DURHAM   302, 463, 491
DU SOSA   640
DUSTBOX   244
DUTCHMAN(MEN)   27, 93, 138,
   162, 171, 175, 202, 208, 214, 250, 263,
   300, 333, 336, 352, 381, 406, 451, 461,
   497, 502, 568, 571, 576, 594, 699, 719,
   729, 776, 778, 803, 831
DUTY   48

DWARF(S)   149, 259, 316, 328, 407,
   447, 452, 470, 512, 526, 588, 594
DWINDLE   523, 632
DYING   322
DYMNUS   223
DYSCOLUS   547
DYSPRAGIA   200
EAGLE(S)   280, 454
EAMBIA   88
EARINA   744
EARINE   618
EARL(S)   257, 366
EAR-LACK   476
EARNEST   364
EARS   385
EARSBY   451
EARTH   202, 208, 317, 324, 366, 381,
   514, 767, 778
EARTHWORM   784
EARTHY SPIRIT(S)   497
EASE   18
EAST WIND   778
EASTER TERM   244
EASY   244
EAUFRIDE   772
EBEA   94
EBROISTEN   364
ECHO(ES)   68, 83, 90, 98, 122, 124,
   137, 162, 164, 181, 183, 225, 231, 238,
   269, 270, 309, 321, 343, 375, 389, 441,
   461, 467, 504, 511, 548, 595, 611, 629,
   633, 654, 685, 709, 772, 790, 797, 821
ECONOMA   353
ECONOMICUS   602
ECPHISTOUN   487
EDELBERT   772
EDELL   740
EDELRED   772
EDGAR   115, 265
EDGWORTH   455
EDIFICATION   59
EDINBURGH   487
EDITH   565, 772
EDMONTON   264, 632, 785
EDMUND   110, 112, 129, 138, 141,
   145, 251, 265, 302, 349, 740, 806, 824
EDOLL   822
EDOMITE(S)   382
EDULF   740

EDWARD   142, 145, 176, 177, 302, 400, 465, 512, 821

EDWARD I OF ENGLAND   112, 520

EDWARD II OF ENGLAND   129

EDWARD III OF ENGLAND   129, 140, 409, 615

EDWARD IV OF ENGLAND   126, 138, 140, 142, 153, 154, 302, 409

EDWARD V OF ENGLAND   126, 142

EDWARD, EARL OF MARCH   119

EDWARD OF ENGLAND   158, 329

EDWARD, PRINCE OF WALES   121, 138, 140, 142, 212, 729

EDWARD THE CONFESSOR   419

EDWIN   822

EGERS   564

EGEUS   170

EGISTUS   468

EGLA   638

EGLAMOUR   391, 618

EGLANTINE   449

EGLON   552

EGMOND   149

EGMONT   192, 256

EGREMONT   515

EGYPT/EGYPTIAN(S)   61, 73, 94, 99, 108, 123, 132, 146, 149, 260, 280, 313, 405, 534, 553, 569, 584, 585, 645, 710, 738, 800

EIRA   553

EIRON   547

EITHERSIDE   457

ELAND   615

ELATION   49

ELBOW   392

ELCHEE   744

ELDER(S)   76.5, 636

ELDER BROTHER(S)   524

ELDORADA   434

ELDRED   740

ELEANOR   101, 112, 119, 121, 174, 179, 180, 246, 302, 411, 520, 722, 801

ELEANOR OF AQUITAINE   398

ELEAZER   777, 823

ELECTOR(S)   329, 729

ELECTRA   42, 200, 202, 468, 485, 683

ELEEMOZYNUS   602

ELEGANCE   181

ELEGANT LOVER(S)   437

ELEMENTS   202, 208, 324, 366, 514, 767, 778

ELENCHI   556

ELENER   556

ELETTO   689

ELEUSIS   602

ELEUTHERIA   200

ELEUTHERIOTES   218

ELF(VES)   201, 548

ELFIRON   241

ELFRIDE   772

ELGINA   740

ELIANOR   722

ELICIA   439

ELIDURUS   229

ELIMINE   146

ELINOR (*SEE* ELEANOR)   112, 174, 179, 180, 520

ELISA   825

ELIZA   83, 629

ELIZABETH   126, 138, 142, 153, 154, 215, 400, 445, 446, 507, 585, 785, 801

ELIZABETH I OF ENGLAND   88, 215, 224, 510

ELKWIN   772

ELLEN   211, 256

ELLENER   556

ELLENORA   626

ELLIS   177

ELNER   113

ELPHISTOUN   487

ELPIDIA   703

ELPINE   417

ELPINO   812

ELPINUS   97

ELRED   531

ELSINGE-SPITTLE   302

ELSINORA   604

ELTHAM   179

ELVIRA   525

ELY   142, 165, 179, 180, 400, 666

ELYDURE   229

EM   113

EMANGOLY   744

EMANUEL   650, 670

EMBRODERADA   434

EMBROIDERER(S)   488

EMERIA   593

EMERSLEY   153

EMILIA (*SEE* AEMILIA)   120, 203,

622, 624, 626, 628, 629, 632, 633, 635.5,
637, 638, 639, 640, 641, 642, 643, 644,
645, 646, 647, 649, 651, 652, 660, 661,
665, 666, 667, 670, 671, 674.5, 679, 680,
681, 682, 683, 684, 688, 689, 691, 693,
699, 700, 701, 702, 704, 705, 707, 708,
709, 712, 715, 718, 719, 720, 721, 722,
723, 724, 725, 726, 727, 730, 746, 748,
750, 751, 758, 759, 760, 761, 763, 768,
770, 771, 773, 776, 778, 785, 794, 796,
799, 802, 803, 804, 806, 807, 808, 810,
814, 815, 818, 821, 823, 824, 825, 826,
827, 829, 831, 836
EPIMELIA   218
EPIRE   277, 294, 380, 444, 572, 766
EPIRUS   444
EPISCOPARIAN   636
EPITON   99
EPPING   591
EQUALITY   367, 383
EQUATO   203
EQUITY   40, 190, 335, 387
ERAS   108, 132
ERASMUS   451, 809
ERASTUS   109, 110
ERATO   58, 83, 89, 106, 156, 164, 202,
208, 344, 365, 366, 407, 411, 414, 437,
487, 527, 731, 732
ERATON   663
ERBAIGH   451
ERCOLE   388
EREBUS-AP-CHAOS-AP-DEMOGOR-
GON-AP-ETERNITY   496
EREMITE(S)   514
ERESTUS   137
ERGASTO   183, 534, 629, 812
ERGASTUS   97, 227, 417
ERIC   604
ERICTHINIS   105
ERICTHO   231, 485
ERINTA   206
ERISICTHON   178
ERISTUS   106
ERITHREA   790
ERKINWALD   740
ERMINHILD   305
ERMSBY   121
ERNESTO   725
ERO   301
EROCLEA   420

EROS   218, 344, 346, 405, 553, 607,
614, 645
EROSTRATO   60
EROTA   648
EROTIA   715
EROTIUM   135
ERPINGHAM   165
ERRAND   31
ERROR   237, 311, 324, 412
ERRORS   335
ERYTHAEA   622
ESAU   51
ESCALUS   143, 392, 395
ESCANES   284
ESCURES   275
ESGUARD   659
ESPERNON   274, 275, 307
ESPILUS   152
ESQUIRE(S)   140, 168, 708
ESSEX   101, 102, 244, 398, 445, 711
ESTAS   421
ESTATES   194, 202, 500, 670
ESTHER   75
ESTIFANIA   598, 723
ESTRILD   136
ESYCHIA   200
ETEOCLES   61
ETERNAL PLAINTIFF   496
ETERNAL UNITY   237
ETERNITY   278, 324, 496
ETERNIZEMENT   835
ETHELRED   740
ETHELSWICK   772
ETHENWALD   115
ETHICUS   353
ETHIOPIA/ETHIOPIAN(S)   (SEE
MOOR(S))   40, 136, 146, 231, 269,
280, 416, 584, 671, 710, 714, 771, 806
ETHNE   593
ETHOS   500
ETHUSA   735
ETON   585
ETRUSCAN(S)   698
EUARCHUS   499, 583
EUBELLA   573
EUBULUS   39, 58, 436, 499, 572, 813
EUCAMPSE   269
EUCHRYSIUS   605
EUCLIA   437
EUCOLOS   181

EUCOSMOS   181
EUCRATIA   619
EUDAIMONIA   200
EUDEMUS   216, 703
EUDINA   807
EUDOCIA   459
EUDORA   301, 537, 735
EUDOXIA   459, 667
EUGENE   619
EUGENIA   228, 386, 462, 479, 661, 669, 707, 717, 766, 777
EUGENIE   304
EUGENIO   26, 330, 384, 534, 704, 802
EUGENIUS   533, 551, 552
EUGENUA   82
EUGENY   784
EULALIA   31, 810
EULINUS   482
EUMELA   701
EUMENA   834
EUMENES   260, 619, 637
EUMENIA   783
EUMENIDES   99, 137
EUMORPHE   458
EUNOMIA (SEE GRACES)   98, 202, 208, 310, 340, 488, 529, 627, 670
EUNUCH(S)   196, 259, 286, 332, 382, 396, 405, 412, 416, 430, 445, 446, 459, 465, 532, 553, 645, 667, 714, 719, 730, 763, 780, 793, 827
EUPANTASTE   181
EUPATHES   181
EUPHANES   663, 738
EUPHATHUS   807
EUPHEMIA   496, 536
EUPHEMUS   437
EUPHORBUS   314
EUPHORIS   269
EUPHRANIA   480
EUPHRASIA   363
EUPHRATA   472
EUPHRATES   794
EUPHRON   108
EUPHRONIUS   405, 553
EUPHROSYNE (SEE GRACES)   100, 146, 164, 200, 202, 208, 271, 346, 613, 791
EUPHUES   384, 784
EUPORIA   202
EURENOSES   458

EURIMONE   567
EURIONE   236, 590, 792
EURISTEUS   317
EURITHEA   506
EURITUS   317
EUROPE   324, 366, 775, 803
EUROTA   105
EURYBATES   42, 146
EURYDICE   450
EURYLOCHUS   537
EURYMEDON   671
EURYMINE   164
EUSANIUS   819
EUSEBEIA   496
EUSEBIUS   78
EUSTACE   149, 211, 333, 457, 515, 749, 817
EUTERPE   58, 83, 89, 156, 164, 202, 208, 344, 365, 366, 407, 411, 414, 437, 487, 527, 731, 732
EUTHALPE   703
EUTHYMIUS   605
EUTOLMOS   181
EVADNE   357, 469, 582
EVAGRIO   560
EVALDUS   690
EVAN   609
EVANDER   694, 738, 766
EVANDRA   684
EVANGELIST(S)   26
EVANGELIUM   24
EVANGELIUN   24
EVANS   187
EVANTHE   665
EVARCHUS   499, 583
EVARNESS   813
EVE   77
EVEMORE   504
EVENT   341
EVERILL   457
EVERYMAN   4
EVIL(S)   349
EVIL ANGEL(S)   118, 205
EVIL COUNSEL   26
EVIL GENIUS   760
EVIL REPORT   76.5
EVIL SPIRIT(S)   489
EVODIUS   578
EXAMPLE   359
EXCESS   11, 545

FERRET   442, 576, 643
FERREX   39
FERRIS   285
FERRYMAN(MEN)   82, 107, 124
FERTILITY   269
FESTE   396
FEU   395
FEVERSHAM   107, 531
FEZ   94, 95, 445, 446, 777
FIAMETTA   508, 536
FIBBIA   624
FIBS   438
FID   587
FIDAMIRA   797
FIDDLE   242
FIDDLE(S)   385
FIDDLER(S)   123, 125, 137, 206, 225,
     250, 257, 292, 320, 334, 386, 442, 456,
     465, 475, 481, 494, 501, 507, 523, 558,
     570, 573, 580, 591, 628, 630, 632, 646,
     666, 693, 697, 707, 708, 711, 766, 773,
     785, 829, 832
FIDDLE STRING MAKER(S)   290
FIDELE   406, 560
FIDELI   241
FIDELIA   92, 178, 479, 783
FIDELIO   243, 300, 461, 567, 581,
     685, 811
FIDELITY   351
FIDELIUS   688, 783
FIDELLA   471, 593
FIDENCE   52
FIDES CHRISTIANA   24
FIDO   163, 481
FIDUCIO   705
FIDUS   68
FIELD BEE   602
FIELD MARSHAL(S)   564
FIEND(S) (SEE DEVIL(S))   399, 458
FIERY SPIRIT(S)   497
FIFE   404
FILATHES   783
FILBON   285
FILCHER   455
FILENA   738
FILENIO   206
FILFORD   582
FILIUS   19
FILLINO   745
FILLISELLA   290

FILLPOT   465
FILOMERINO   689
FIN   274, 275
FINDLAW   193
FINE   796
FINER(S)   295
FINGERLOCK   204
FINIO   281
FINSBURY   220
FIORETTA   501, 726
FIORINDA   505
FIORMONDA   478
FIRE   202, 208, 324, 366, 514, 527,
     767, 778
FIRENZO   582
FIRIFACIO   434
FIRKE   175
FIRST DOG DAY   358
FISHER   673
FISHERMAN(MEN)   103, 178, 210,
     284, 335, 443, 503, 731, 732, 787, 819
FISHMONGER(S)   96, 114, 335
FISHMONGERS' COMPANY   302,
     332, 466
FISHWOMAN(WOMEN)   748
FISKE   565
FITCHOW   463
FITTON   456
FITZALE   411, 613
FITZALLARD   298
FITZALLEN   352
FITZALWINE   332
FITZAMOROUS   521
FITZAVARICE   521
FITZDOTTRELL   457
FITZGERRARD   718
FITZGRAVE   266
FITZSWORD   176
FITZWATER   141, 179, 180, 329, 749
FITZWORD   176
FIVE SENSES   202, 208, 239, 311,
     335, 496, 514
FIVE STARCHES   365
FIVE WITS   4
FLACCUS   122, 296
FLACILLA   459
FLAG BEARER(S) (SEE ENSIGN(S))
     482
FLAMBIO   633
FLAMETTA   796

FLAMETTE   738
FLAMINEO   268, 306
FLAMINIUS   1, 2, 156, 283, 402, 513
FLANDERS (*SEE* FLEMING(S))
    210, 643
FLASH   195, 217
FLATTERER(S) (*SEE* SYCOPHANT(S))
    229, 252, 410, 689, 720
FLATTERY   43, 193, 194, 434, 547
FLAVANDA   685
FLAVELLO   810
FLAVIA   184, 283, 330, 519, 532, 597,
    719, 741
FLAVIANO   726
FLAVIANUS   765
FLAVIO   532
FLAVIUS   199, 392, 402, 403, 410
FLAWNE   177
FLEANCE   404
FLEBISHITEN   57
FLEDWIT   597
FLEIRE   255
FLEMING   50, 686
FLEMING(S) (*SEE* FLANDERS)
    50, 111, 114, 171, 175, 643
FLESH-HOOK   821
FLEURY   275
FLEXIBILITY   269
FLOOD   154
FLOOD(S)   452
FLORA   83, 207, 238, 339, 376, 377,
    378, 421, 449, 544, 602, 689
FLORADELLA   744
FLORAMELL   329
FLORELIA   726
FLORELIO   811
FLORELLI   747
FLORELLO   428, 802, 833
FLORELLUS   539
FLORENCE (*PROPER NAME*)   211,
    337, 670
FLORENCE   139, 255, 286, 306, 395,
    446, 493, 498, 501, 505, 508, 532, 538,
    621, 664, 736, 774, 782, 796
FLORENTINE(S)   168, 176, 184, 185,
    189, 203, 224, 254, 286, 379, 395, 428,
    445, 446, 475, 479, 490, 493, 506, 577,
    659, 664, 668, 707, 758, 782, 796, 833
FLORENTIO   588
FLORES   169, 712

FLOREZ   643
FLORIA   532
FLORIANA   588
FLORIDA   255, 557, 600
FLORIDA/FLORIDAN(S)   320
FLORILA   159
FLORILLA   626
FLORIMELL   241, 268, 464, 653
FLORIMELLA   268
FLORINA   701
FLORINDA   599
FLORIO   277, 486, 498
FLORIUS   729
FLORIZEL   397
FLOSCULA   99
FLOURISHING   202
FLOWER   242
FLOWERDALE   222
FLOWERDEW   547
FLUELLEN   165
FLUELLO   204
FLUTE   170
FLUTIST(S)   216
FLUTTERKIN   354
FLY   442
FLY-BLOW   709
FLYLOVE   773
FO DE KING   177
FOEMIUS   497
FOGGE   154
FOGGO   206
FOIS   254
FOLIO   578
FOLLY   5, 11, 124, 181, 194, 230, 344,
    349, 586, 711, 713, 767, 835
FOLLYWIT   276
FOND   217
FONDLING   481
FONDNESS   11
FONTINELLE   188, 435
FOOK   688
FOOL(S) (*SEE* CLOWN(S))   33, 69,
    121, 149, 177, 185, 193, 198, 203, 212,
    230, 252, 259, 265, 309, 327, 329, 344,
    394, 395, 396, 402, 453, 478, 497, 537,
    545, 586, 601, 603, 637, 652, 654, 657,
    658, 665, 668, 711, 712, 717, 721, 741,
    742, 772, 778, 810, 824
FOOLE   304
FOOTBALL PLAYER(S)   465

FOOTMAN(MEN) 112, 217, 241, 264, 276, 302, 310, 318, 347, 356, 435, 462, 477, 488, 517, 568, 644, 681, 706, 722, 766, 778, 809, 815, 829

FOOTWELL 721

FOPP 666

FORCE 349

FORD 187

FOREMAN 175

FOREMAN(MEN) 175

FOREMAN OF THE GRAND INQUEST 496

FOREST 126, 739

FORESTE 427

FORESTER(S) (*SEE* WOODMAN(MEN)) 150, 152, 178, 210, 325, 333, 394, 407, 613, 618, 729, 767

FORGIO 661

FORMAL 176, 591, 692

FORMIDON 690

FORMIO 534

FOROBOSCO 184, 185, 389, 668

FORREST 154, 826

FORSA 139

FORSET 445, 446

FORTE 368

FORTINBRAS 197

FORTITUDE 21.5, 202, 208, 290, 335, 355, 383, 409, 434, 483, 495, 500, 514, 786

FORTRESS 594

FORTUNATA 353

FORTUNATUS 162, 234

FORTUNE (*PROPER NAME*) 177

FORTUNE 53, 61, 76, 92, 100, 109, 159, 162, 190, 202, 208, 327, 351, 496, 572, 614, 634, 729, 767, 788, 815

FORTUNE TELLER(S) 125, 251, 353, 534, 535, 585, 649, 708, 724, 779

FORTUNIO 86, 139, 219

FOSCARI 315, 429, 577, 833

FOSSE 706

FOSTER 460, 739

FOULWEATHER 228

FOUL-WEATHER-IN-HARVEST 473

FOUNTAIN 452, 563

FOUR SEASONS 313, 366, 376, 419, 503, 529, 566, 767

FOURCHER 290

FOWLE 107

FOWLER 477

FOX 323, 451, 491

FOXSTONE 262

FOY 157, 445, 809

FOYES 159

FRAILTY 251

FRAILWARE 501

FRAMPUL 442

FRANCA 333

FRANCE (*SEE* FRENCHMAN(MEN)) 101, 102, 133, 138, 140, 148, 150, 154, 162, 165, 171, 180, 202, 208, 210, 212, 213, 241, 246, 254, 265, 274, 275, 307, 329, 333, 365, 368, 395, 398, 399, 503, 545, 550, 649, 714

FRANCELIA 621, 811

FRANCELIA/FRANCELIAN(S) 628

FRANCES 153, 222, 251, 292, 442, 457, 585, 592, 643, 722, 809

FRANCIS 143, 145, 161, 167, 168, 170, 187, 217, 219, 224, 249, 254, 258, 323, 409, 456, 474, 507, 558, 568, 585, 681, 739, 798, 816, 821

FRANCIS I OF FRANCE 550

FRANCISCA 392, 808

FRANCISCAN(S) 143, 306

FRANCISCHINA 214, 297, 437, 724

FRANCISCO 197, 252, 268, 281, 300, 306, 384, 386, 390, 423, 430, 558, 560, 563, 600, 646, 669, 705, 717, 719, 723, 757, 816

FRANCISCUS 580, 712

FRANCISSINA 245

FRANCO 139

FRANCOLIN 571

FRANGIPAN 590

FRANIO 653

FRANK 153, 161, 187, 217, 222, 242, 249, 251, 257, 264, 276, 297, 323, 336, 356, 442, 456, 462, 474, 477, 517, 523, 540, 549, 558, 563, 568, 574, 592, 642, 690, 702, 722, 739, 773, 785, 801, 808, 816, 821, 830

FRANKFORD 258, 817

FRANKLIN 384, 821

FRANKLIN(S) 72, 107

FRANTIC(S) 319

FRANVILLE 656

FRAPOLO 724

FRAPPATORE 230

FRAU   222
FRAUD   85, 93, 349
FREDELINE   506
FREDERICK   95, 121, 162, 171, 205,
    225, 299, 300, 364, 394, 472, 518, 564,
    604, 642, 646, 658, 665, 707, 720, 729,
    742, 773, 835
FREDERICO   498, 599
FREDERIGO   742
FREDIGOND   714
FREDOCALDO   443
FREE WILL   3, 11, 63
FREED MAN(MEN)   12, 316, 410,
    415, 424
FREEDOM   262
FREEMAN   784, 825
FREEMASON(S)   614
FREEVILL   214
FREEWIT   591, 594
FRENCHMAN(MEN) *(SEE* FRANCE)
    49, 85, 93, 109, 111, 119, 122, 123, 129,
    149, 159, 162, 165, 166, 169, 171, 177,
    187, 188, 205, 212, 214, 224, 225, 228,
    252, 274, 275, 281, 293, 306, 310, 329,
    333, 336, 351, 394, 395, 399, 400, 406,
    418, 438, 445, 464, 475, 490, 491, 502,
    508, 510, 515, 549, 555, 558, 559, 565,
    568, 576, 582, 639, 640, 641, 644, 653,
    656, 659, 662, 689, 692, 706, 714, 715,
    719, 722, 741, 759, 763, 767, 773, 776,
    809, 821
FRESCO   293
FRESCOBALD   189
FRESCOBALDI   254
FRESH CHEESE AND CREAM
    WOMAN(WOMEN)
    799
FRESHWATER   549
FRESOLIN   621
FRESSINGFIELD   121
FRET   614
FRETELYNE   320
FRIAR(S)   14, 24, 32, 100, 101, 102,
    112, 121, 133, 137, 143, 154, 168, 179,
    180, 188, 193, 194, 204, 205, 211, 215,
    241, 246, 254, 264, 283, 286, 305, 306,
    315, 332, 362, 388, 392, 440, 459, 470,
    475, 478, 486, 490, 508, 520, 561, 565,
    618, 649, 665, 669, 670, 689, 715, 719,
    726, 747, 760, 774, 777, 810, 811, 816,
    826

FRICASE   802
FRIDLAND   564
FRIEND(S)   116, 121, 217, 352, 410,
    477, 492, 560, 562, 779
FRIENDLESS   72
FRIENDLY   722, 776, 825
FRIENDSHIP   41, 434, 823
FRIGOSO   670
FRION   491
FRIPPER   236
FRIPPERY   266
FRISCO   164, 188, 336
FRISCOBALDO   435
FRISK   549
FRISKIBALL   189
FRISKIN   624
FRISWOOD   587
FRITH   361
FRIVOLO   684
FRIZ   492
FROBISHER   224, 409
FROG   211
FROG(S)   503
FROLIC   137, 776
FROLLO   422, 604
FROMAGA   255
FRONIA   89
FRONTO   444
FROTH   392, 474
FROW   419
FROY   456
FRUGAL   788
FRUGALITY   59, 434
FRUIT BEARER(S)   798
FRUIT SELLER(S)   407
FRUITFUL   784
FRUITION   738
FUB   580
FUCATO   243
FUCUS   602
FUENTE   723
FUENTES   440
FUGA   746
FUGITIVE(S)   418
FUGITIVE FAVORITE   454
FULBANK   473
FULCINIUS   216, 424
FULGENS   1
FULGENTIO   470, 582
FULGOSO   555
FULK   266

FULL MOON   250
FULLER   191
FULLER(S)   125, 495
FULSOME   286, 697
FULVIA   97, 122, 296, 554, 698
FULVIO   479, 742
FULVIUS   296, 667
FUMANTE   774
FUMBLE   507
FUND-JONET   193
FUNGOSO   163, 599
FUNGUS   226
FURBISHER   224, 409
FURBO   330
FURIES (*SEE* ALECTO, MEGAERA,
    TYSIPHONE)   39, 89, 92, 104,
    122, 127, 137, 155, 305, 317, 382, 431,
    489, 498, 504, 514, 527, 554, 571, 574,
    578, 599, 670, 673, 675, 688, 703, 731,
    732, 826
FURIO   198
FURIOSO   361, 441
FURIOUS   831
FURNACE   474
FURNIFALL   228
FUROR POETICUS   225, 836
FURTHERANCE   70
FURTIVO   243
FURY   89, 280, 290, 302, 313, 319,
    325, 390, 443
FUSCUS   186
FUSTIAN WEAVER(S)   815
FUSTIGO   204
FUTELLI   555
FYNDLAW   193
GABETZA   230
GABINIUS   296, 444
GABRIEL   138, 720, 808
GABRIELLA   670, 809
GADSHILL   145, 148
GAETULIA/GAETULIAN(S)   128
GAGE   215
GAINSFORD   220
GAIUS   1, 2
GALANTIS   317
GALATEA   105, 363, 407, 526, 695
GALBA   410
GALD   327
GALEATZO   184, 185
GALEAZZO   418, 758

GALEOTTO   599, 624
GALIARBUS   69
GALILEE   579
GALLA   296, 698
GALLANT(S)   35, 49, 93, 150, 188,
    195, 198, 214, 239, 242, 263, 266, 267,
    295, 321, 323, 420, 422, 427, 428, 429,
    440, 442, 456, 457, 461, 462, 463, 472,
    477, 478, 479, 480, 481, 484, 488, 494,
    498, 507, 508, 515, 516, 517, 518, 519,
    520, 521, 523, 532, 534, 535, 536, 540,
    541, 542, 545, 547, 549, 551, 552, 555,
    559, 562, 563, 568, 570, 573, 575, 582,
    584, 586, 587, 588, 589, 590, 591, 592,
    594, 601, 616, 617, 621, 624, 628, 632,
    641, 646, 652, 656, 661, 666, 668, 671,
    681, 684, 693, 699, 701, 705, 707, 708,
    711, 714, 718, 719, 720, 721, 722, 723,
    724, 747, 752, 759, 760, 771, 772, 773,
    780, 806, 808, 809, 817, 829, 832
GALLAS   564
GALLATHEA   105, 363, 407, 526,
    695
GALLERIUS   802
GALLIA   213, 729
GALLIARD   692, 809
GALLICUS   327
GALLIGASKEN   434
GALLIPOT   298
GALLIPUS   619
GALLOP   300
GALLOWAY   112, 162
GALLUS   132, 186, 216, 240, 312,
    320, 405, 553
GALOSHIO   652
GAMALIEL   623
GAMBOLL   606
GAME, MASTER OF   835
GAMEKEEPER(S)   15, 652
GAMELIA   237
GAMESTER(S)   222, 272, 303, 414,
    442, 455, 460, 488, 496, 523, 535, 570,
    611, 702, 762
GAMMER GURTON   67
GANDOLPHO   624
GANIO   73, 74
GANYCTOR   701
GANYMEDE   128, 144, 186, 294, 298,
    317, 394, 465, 782
GARD   706

61

GEOMETRY   202, 208, 290, 302, 322,
  421, 670, 731, 732
GEORGE   119, 126, 138, 142, 154,
  155, 158, 163, 168, 176, 180, 187, 202,
  204, 215, 220, 234, 244, 251, 256, 262,
  282, 285, 288, 302, 316, 460, 477, 487,
  496, 540, 545, 585, 606, 618, 632, 680,
  718, 729, 740, 749, 821
GEORGIO   435, 747
GERALDINE   323, 484
GERARD   423, 462, 643, 670, 757
GERARDINE   263
GERASTO   653
GERILLO   206
GERMAN(S) (*SEE* GERMANY)   49,
  162, 257, 604, 719, 763, 815
GERMANE   510
GERMANICUS   240
GERMANUS   815
GERMANY (*SEE* GERMAN(S))
  121, 162, 205, 212, 329, 364, 386, 472,
  564, 729
GERMINATIO   270
GERO   206
GERON   99, 414, 807
GERONTUS   85
GERROLD   492
GERTREDE   197
GERTRID   520
GERTRUDE   197, 217, 643
GERVASE   323, 462, 512, 585
GERVORON   791
GETA   380, 554, 654
GETICA   283
GETTALL   788
GETTINGS   473
GHOST(S) (*SEE* SPIRIT(S))   28, 29,
  45, 76.5, 89, 110, 126, 127, 136, 137, 142,
  154, 156, 178, 185, 197, 221, 231, 232,
  240, 246, 254, 260, 285, 293, 296, 305,
  306, 307, 314, 316, 317, 332, 350, 382,
  403, 404, 406, 418, 424, 447, 455, 458,
  468, 469, 475, 482, 485, 489, 510, 520,
  534, 545, 554, 559, 574, 578, 599, 605,
  612, 649, 672, 675, 688, 698, 699, 703,
  712, 714, 715, 736, 744, 772, 779, 785,
  802, 823, 826
GIACOMO   296
GIACOPE   478
GIANETTA   206

GIANT(S)   55, 218, 233, 302, 316, 366,
  453, 514, 526, 545
GIBIUS   444
GIBLETS   407
GIFT   606
GILBERT   112, 158, 179, 180, 254,
  400, 409, 515, 587, 778, 801, 826
GILBERTY   582
GILDAS   89
GILDERSTONE   197
GILES   228, 474, 491, 592, 835
GILIAN   494
GILL   653, 801
GILLA   89
GILLAMOR   89
GILLIAN   220, 494, 632, 646, 653, 691
GILTHEAD   457
GINET   507
GINGERBREAD WOMAN(WOMEN)
  455
GINGLE   414
GINKES   643
GINNY   262
GIORDANO   306
GIOTTO   429, 577
GIOVANELLO   297
GIOVANNI   203, 306, 386, 418, 486,
  505, 582, 724, 747, 816
GIOVANNO   582
GIPTIAN(S)   73
GIRALDO   653
GIRO   206
GIRPIDES   422
GISBERT   565, 741
GISBERTUS   78
GISCO   231
GISGON   513
GISMOND   104, 254, 300
GIULIANO   176
GLADIATOR(S)   314, 453
GLADIOLUS   449
GLADNESS   200, 202, 208, 434
GLAMIS   404
GLANSDALE   399
GLASCOT   520
GLASIER(S)   613
GLASTONBURY   826
GLAUCE   269
GLAUCILLA   443
GLAUCUS   437, 443, 553

GUIDERIUS   406, 551, 552
GUIDO   315, 364, 538
GUILDENSTERN   197
GUILDFORD   256, 400
GUILFRIDO   88
GUILT   434
GUIMANTES   551, 552
GUINEVERE   89, 299, 327
GUIOMAR   640
GUISE   133, 246, 307
GUISHARD   104
GULATO   361
GULCH   188, 290
GULF   262
GULL(S)   176, 214, 245, 297, 298, 420,
   425, 428, 436, 441, 463, 465, 477, 479,
   481, 484, 507, 517, 519, 521, 538, 548,
   549, 556, 562, 568, 575, 577, 583, 587,
   593, 594, 597, 599, 632, 641, 642, 681,
   693, 702, 703, 708, 721, 724, 725, 736,
   759, 762, 778, 796, 808, 809, 829
GULLMAN   276
GULMAN   741
GUMB   799
GUMWATER   276
GUNNER(S)   77, 192, 218, 241, 248,
   355, 399, 500, 502, 657, 739
GUNOPHILUS   144
GUNWATER   276
GURGUNT   75
GURNEY   129, 398
GURTON   67
GUSTUS   4, 202, 208, 239, 311, 335,
   496, 514
GUTT   290
GUY   129, 298, 305, 333, 496, 818
GUYAMARA   717
GUZMAN   555
GWALTER   198
GWENARD   39
GWENTHYAN   198
GYB   67
GYMCRACK   718
GYMNOSOPHIST(S)   584
GYNECIA   583
GYNETIA   235
GYNRN   609
GYPSY(IES)   353, 496, 547, 585, 708,
   717, 779, 781, 836
GYPTES   99

HABERDASHER(S)   120, 163, 224,
   333, 456, 481, 522, 547
HABERDASHERS' COMPANY
   302, 332, 466
HABITS AND MANNERS, MASTER
   OF   459
HABREN   136
HACKNEYMAN(MEN)   125
HACKSTER(S)   73
HADDIT   321
HADES   404
HADLAND   153, 762, 801
HADRIANOPLE   793
HAEBE   105
HAEMON   450
HAG(S) (SEE WITCH(ES))   280, 404,
   450
HAGGIS   455
HAIMANTUS   537
HAINAULT   129
HAIRCUT   518
HAL   145, 165, 167
HALA   489
HALBERDIER(S)   110, 142, 155, 189,
   203, 214, 272, 277, 295, 310, 335, 418,
   486, 626, 785, 835
HALEB   109
HALES   189
HALFERIGGE   520
HALFPENNY   125
HALI   130, 248, 622, 763, 780, 827
HALICLYON   407
HALISDUS   685
HALLIBECK   248
HALTERSACKE   48
HALY   130, 248, 622, 763, 780, 827
HAMAN   33
HAMBRE   669
HAMDON   220
HAMET   127, 220
HAMILTON   585, 680
HAMLET   197, 217
HAMLUC   785
HAMMERSHIN   465
HAMMERTON   316
HAMMON   175
HAMMOND   672
HAMON   33, 447
HAMOND   565
HAMPSHIRE   323, 740

HAMPSTEAD 617
HAMPTON 496
HAMZE 744
HANAN 51
HANCE 27, 50
HANDSAW 382
HANGER 298
HANGER(S)-ON 334
HANGMAN(MEN) (*SEE*
    EXECUTIONER(S)) 50, 58,
    73, 110, 154, 182, 189, 275, 380, 424,
    716, 719, 739, 801
HANKIN 50
HANNA 799
HANNAH 809
HANNECKE 354
HANNIBAL 513, 617
HANNO 513
HANNO MAGNUS 231
HANON 160
HANS 27, 50, 169, 175, 250, 257, 354,
    456, 729, 831
HAPCE 126
HAPHAZARD 65
HAPSBURG 215
HARALDUS 752
HARCOP 249
HARCOURT 167
HARDENBERGH 169
HARDING 739
HARDY DARDY 33
HARDYMAN 809
HARE(S) 454
HAREBRAIN 276, 563
HARFLEUR 165
HARGRAVE 494
HARINGFIELD 535
HARLATE 631
HARLAY 275
HARLEQUIN 248, 526
HARLING 801
HARLOTTO 631
HARMAN 192
HARMANTS 354
HARMONIA 270, 694
HARMONY 324, 351, 358, 367, 407,
    411, 453, 454, 488, 586, 607, 731
HARPAGUS 209
HARPASTES 537
HARPAX 46, 330, 380

HARPER 256
HARPER(S) 112, 327, 411, 466, 482,
    566, 609
HARPOOLE 166
HARPY(IES) 390, 496
HARQUEBUSIER(S) 39
HARROLD 604, 740
HARROW 455
HARRY 119, 141, 145, 148, 153, 155,
    165, 166, 167, 182, 220, 256, 262, 264,
    323, 329, 334, 400, 456, 535, 585, 594,
    635.5, 672, 673, 808
HART(S) 754, 806, 816
HARTWELL 563, 592
HARVEST 173
HARVEST MAN(MEN) (*SEE*
    REAPER(S)) 137, 290
HARVEY 145, 336, 826
HASLERIGG 520
HASMOND 604
HASTINGS 126, 138, 142, 167, 400
HATERIUS 216
HATRED 434
HATTER(S) 456, 792
HATTO 472
HATTON 585
HATUN 458
HAUGHTY 304
HAUVRYE 192
HAVE-AT-ALL 702
HAVE-LITTLE 255
HAVER 425
HAWK(S) 11
HAWKER(S) 772
HAWKINS 409
HAWKWOOD 409
HAXTER 802
HAZZARD 220, 523
HEADBOROUGH(S) 168, 617
HEADSMAN(MEN) (*SEE*
    EXECUTIONER(S)) 153,
    171, 256, 393, 446, 578, 714
HEALTH 27, 566, 572, 767
HEARE-SAY 702
HEARING 4, 202, 208, 239, 311, 335,
    496, 514
HEART 383
HEART-HOLE 635.5
HEARTLESS 802
HEARTLOVE 574

HOBS   153
HOBSON   224
HODGE   48, 67, 161, 175, 189, 442,
   460, 635.5, 817
HOEL   89
HOFA   780
HOFFMAN   438, 740
HOG   321, 825
HOG(S)   454
HOGREL   407
HOGSDON   176, 535, 773
HOLBORN   298, 835
HOLD   323
HOLDFAST   217, 591, 788
HOLDUP   463
HOLIFERNES   150, 214, 252
HOLINESS   43
HOLLAND   119, 568, 680
HOLLANDER(S) (*SEE* DUTCHMAN
   (MEN))   138, 461
HOLLARO   791
HOLMES   256
HOLOFERNES   150, 214, 252
HOLY GHOST   306
HOLY ROMAN EMPIRE (*SEE*
   GERMANY)   241
HOLY-HOCKE   587
HOLYWATER   721
HOMELINESS   193
HOMER   294, 313, 317, 497
HOMICIDE   182
HOMILY   836
HOMO   17, 18
HOMONOIA   496
HONEST INDUSTRY   93
HONESTY   41, 115, 215, 224, 473,
   670, 699
HONEYSUCKLE   257
HONORA   647
HONORATUS   410
HONOREA   826
HONORIA   436, 473, 549, 560
HONORIO   297, 597, 726, 774
HONOUR   47, 50, 93, 100, 181, 310,
   335, 351, 356, 383, 387, 413, 419, 448,
   473, 487, 495, 572, 670, 786, 835
HOOD   32, 158, 174, 179, 180, 332, 618
HOOD(S)   613
HOOK   465
HOOP   617

HOPE   11, 100, 104, 338, 355, 367,
   434, 448, 483, 514, 546, 665, 738, 746,
   786
HORACE   186, 195
HORATIO   110, 197, 221, 228, 267,
   273, 519, 536, 582, 719, 733, 796, 810
HORATIUS   61, 273, 765
HORESTES   48
HORMENUS   752
HORNE   630, 631, 697
HORNER   15, 119
HORNET   250, 592, 602
HOROLOGUS   605
HORROR   78, 290
HORROR OF MIND   78
HORSE(S)   109, 173, 190, 404, 452,
   494, 526
HORSE, MASTER OF   389, 533
HORSE-CORSER(S)   205, 455
HORSELEECH   435
HORSEMAN(MEN)   129, 186, 318,
   488, 660
HORSUS   815
HORTANO   361
HORTEN   576
HORTENSIA   362, 796
HORTENSIO   120, 268, 306, 726, 758
HORTENSIUS   402, 605
HORTENZO   777
HOSA   780
HOSCHERMAN   169
HOSPITABLE BEE   602
HOSPITAL, MASTER OF   153
HOSPITALITY   85
HOST(S) (*SEE* TAVERNER(S))   12,
   60, 126, 159, 166, 171, 187, 189, 190,
   262, 264, 283, 309, 316, 354, 364, 391,
   442, 460, 474, 481, 488, 494, 516, 521,
   561, 568, 575, 642, 649, 651, 668, 669,
   711, 713, 739, 780, 799, 806
HOSTAGE(S)   567
HOSTESS(ES)   120, 121, 137, 145,
   165, 167, 187, 190, 205, 250, 283, 290,
   309, 337, 445, 474, 481, 494, 540, 544,
   561, 568, 668, 669, 717, 748, 773
HOSTILITY   355
HOSTILIUS   402, 823
HOSTLER(S)   145, 166, 205, 264, 361,
   442, 669
HOTSPUR   141, 145

HOUND(S)   264, 390, 454, 494
HOUR(S)   238, 313, 607
HOURS   98, 202, 208, 340, 488, 527,
    529, 627, 670
HOUSEHOLD GOD(S)   339
HOUSEKEEPER(S)   182, 303, 508,
    787, 798
HOWARD   153, 154, 215
HOWDEE   463
HOWELL   129, 531, 609
HOWLEGLASS   411
HOWLET   808
HOYDEN   587
HOYST   788
HUANEBANGO   137
HUBBA   136, 604
HUBERT   101, 102, 180, 214, 398,
    533, 643, 749
HUDE   332
HUET   215
HUFF   56
HUFFLE   442
HUGH   112, 129, 138, 143, 168, 175,
    179, 180, 187, 191, 451, 460, 476, 531,
    542, 587, 617, 632, 656, 680, 688, 773
HUGHBALL   586
HUGO   465
HUGUENOT(S)   133
HULACUS   482
HULDRICK   531, 740
HULVERHEAD   806
HUMAN DISCOURSE   63
HUMANITAS   193, 194
HUMANITY   6, 500
HUMBER   136, 218, 419
HUMBLE BEE   602
HUME   119
HUMES   158
HUMIL   285
HUMILIATION   678.5
HUMILITY   7, 18, 20, 43, 72, 434,
    466, 546, 670
HUMOR   767
HUMOURS (SEE COMPLEXIONS)
    237, 767
HUMPHREY   119, 153, 155, 165, 167,
    174, 242, 302, 316, 399, 409, 455, 463,
    563, 613, 722, 801
HUNGARY/HUNGARIAN(S)   74,
    95, 205, 306, 436, 564
HUNGER   608

HUNSDON   224, 451
HUNTING   731, 732
HUNTINGTON   166, 174, 179, 180,
    256, 332, 520
HUNTLEY   491
HUNTLOVE   681
HUNTRESS(ES)   294, 313, 317, 366,
    499
HUNTSMAN(MEN)   15, 51, 83, 106,
    120, 138, 149, 153, 163, 170, 173, 174,
    175, 183, 187, 198, 201, 226, 235, 258,
    262, 313, 315, 332, 361, 368, 385, 394,
    423, 459, 488, 492, 493, 494, 514, 533,
    541, 618, 629, 643, 652, 729, 754, 768,
    787, 825
HURRY   523
HURSLY   126
HURTFUL HELP   70
HUSBAND(S)   272, 356
HUSBANDMAN(MEN)   125, 178
HUSBANDRY   731, 732
HUSON   688
HYACINTH   376, 378
HYADES   309
HYANTHE   169, 537
HYARCHUS   314
HYDARNES   570
HYDASPES   328, 584
HYDASPUS   744
HYDE PARK   517
HYDROPHOBIA   420
HYLACE   539
HYLAS   499, 558, 695
HYLUS   301
HYMEN   110, 237, 271, 300, 325, 346,
    394, 437, 492, 560, 614, 627, 633, 731,
    732, 759, 771, 782, 796, 825
HYPARCHA   648
HYPERBOLUS   469
HYPERCRITIC OF MANNERS   496
HYPERIA   735
HYPERION   294
HYPOCRISIS   24
HYPOCRISY   41, 59, 78, 237, 290
HYPODAMIA   317
HYPOMENE   218
HYPSICRATEA   280
HYRCANIA   744
HYTHE   400
IACHIMO   406
IAGO   362, 379, 440

IANTHE   146, 269, 301, 763, 827
IANTHUS   450
IBERIA/IBERIAN(S)   360, 444, 583,
    813
ICELES   527
ICENI/ICENIAN(S)   280, 655
ICETIS   694
ICILIUS   733
IDA   149
IDEM   241
IDEN   119
IDLE   251
IDLENESS   26, 53, 55
IDLESBY   697
IDMON   381
IDOL(S)   454, 593
IDOLATRY   24
IDUMEUS   48
IFFIDA   744
IGNATIUS   412
IGNIS   366
IGNIS FATUUS   527
IGNORANCE   6, 53, 55, 57, 59, 100,
    280, 302, 311, 344, 349, 362, 454
IGNORANT ASS   504
IGNORATIO ELENCHI   556
IGNORATIO ELENER   556
ILFORD   249
ILIGI   448
ILIONEUS   128
ILL   489
ILL MAY DAY   358
ILL REPORT   76.5
ILL WILL   27
ILLAWE   564
ILLIBEGGE   458
ILLIBERAL LOVER(S)   437
ILLYRIA/ILLYRIAN(S)   95, 396
ILTRISTE   602
IMAGINATION   3
IMMODEST   545
IMMODESTY   434
IMMERITO   225
IMOGEN   406
IMPARTIALITY   383
IMPATIENT POVERTY   30
IMPERFECT CREATURE(S)   348
IMPERIA   188
IMPERIALE   560
IMPIETY   53, 635
IMPLEMENT   414

IMPORTUNITY   40
IMPOSTOR(S)   119, 449, 461
IMPOSTURE   526
IMPOTENS   602
IMPUDENCE   181, 280, 311, 434, 547
IN AND IN   617
INA   124
INACHUS   528
INAMORATO   602
INCA(NS)   787
INCHIQUIN   686
INCLE   290
INCLINATION   49
INCONSIDERATION   57
INCONTINENCE   53, 688
INCORRIGIBLE   697
INCUBO   669
INDAMORA   497
INDEPENDANT(S)   636, 673, 679
INDIA   94, 295, 351, 383
INDIAN(S)   123, 149, 170, 295, 310,
    351, 383, 421, 454, 466, 497, 502, 546,
    566, 670, 788, 800
INDIAN(S) OF AMERICA   310, 320,
    487, 803
INDIAN(S) OF PERU   787
INDIFFERENT DAYS   358
INDIGENCE   52
INDIGENT POVERTY   52
IN-DOCK-OUT-NETTLE   358
INDUCTION   1, 2, 39, 61, 64, 89, 92,
    104, 109, 110, 120, 126, 128, 136, 137,
    149, 151, 155, 156, 162, 163, 171, 173,
    177, 179, 181, 182, 184, 186, 203, 221,
    225, 231, 234, 235, 241, 244, 248, 252,
    254, 264, 287, 305, 316, 325, 327, 333,
    365, 412, 414, 431, 455, 456, 457, 465,
    481, 482, 501, 504, 537, 547, 548, 554,
    567, 616, 670, 674, 699, 761, 787, 798,
    802, 824, 826, 836
INDUCTOR(S)   806
INDULGENCE   89, 414, 434
INDUSTRY   93, 302, 351, 367, 409,
    419, 448, 670, 786
INESSE   276
INFAELICITO   361
INFANS   5
INFANTA(S)   456, 525, 596, 728, 777
INFELICHE   204, 435
INFELICHI   581
INFESTO   243

73

JOSALIN   802
JOSEPH   120, 362, 382, 535, 710, 823
JOSEPH OF ARIMATHEA   579
JOSEPHUS   382, 823
JOSHUA   365, 510
JOSINA   721
JOSSELIN   153, 154
JOURDAIN   119
JOURNEYMAN(MEN)   175, 204,
    440, 531
JOVANI   816
JOVE   64, 294, 365, 381, 421, 437, 453,
    454, 458, 487, 496, 528, 593, 699, 796,
    805
JOVIAL LOVER(S)   437
JOVINELLI   305
JOVIO   386, 742
JOY   64, 104, 288, 434, 613, 738
JOYCE   262, 323, 516, 617, 672, 673,
    809
JOYEUX   133
JOYLESS   586
JOYNTURE   831
JUAN   598
JUANNA   490, 717
JUDA   40, 382
JUDAH   579, 710
JUDAS   72, 579, 655
JUDAS MACCABEUS   150, 365
JUDEA/JUDEAN(S)   308
JUDEX   76.5
JUDGE(S) (*SEE* JUSTICE(S))   31,
    50, 56, 65, 76.5, 85, 115, 117, 118, 134,
    148, 166, 190, 244, 253, 255, 265, 275,
    293, 317, 337, 353, 362, 364, 366, 388,
    400, 414, 419, 442, 456, 464, 495, 514,
    550, 559, 560, 582, 584, 586, 605, 619,
    628, 638, 639, 661, 673, 711, 733, 783,
    806, 810
JUDGEMENT   24, 47, 53, 295
JUDICIOUS LOVER(S)   437
JUDICIUM   556
JUDICO   225
JUDITH   75, 257
JUG   414, 433, 442, 494, 512, 826
JUGA   237
JUGGLER   35, 234
JUGGLER(S)   327, 385, 565, 573, 611,
    643
JUGURTH   231, 382
JULETTA   656, 658

JULIA   147, 186, 198, 240, 245, 286,
    364, 389, 391, 418, 424, 472, 478, 493,
    501, 554, 601, 640, 714, 733, 765, 774
JULIAN   192
JULIANA   157, 393, 657, 668, 726
JULIANO   418, 434
JULIANUS   380, 471
JULIET   143, 392
JULIETTA   392, 517, 742
JULIO   104, 109, 185, 226, 235, 254,
    267, 268, 306, 386, 388, 436, 519, 532,
    575, 580, 642, 653, 728, 736, 742, 758
JULIPPE   802
JULIUS   116, 216, 232, 240, 261, 283,
    296, 365, 387, 403, 444, 482, 645, 698,
    729
JUNIPER   281
JUNIUS   122, 273, 401, 424, 655
JUNO   34, 75, 83, 92, 124, 128, 144,
    164, 186, 207, 237, 261, 294, 313, 317,
    390, 437, 452, 458, 500, 528, 537, 592,
    627, 653, 731, 732, 759, 782
JUPITER   15, 75, 83, 92, 124, 128,
    144, 186, 237, 294, 309, 313, 317, 319,
    355, 365, 380, 387, 406, 411, 437, 454,
    458, 479, 487, 528, 571, 593, 595, 670,
    699, 720, 731, 732, 796
JURY   516, 673
JUST   49, 64, 805
JUST GOVERNMENT   634
JUSTA   500
JUSTICE   21.5, 38, 47, 65, 98, 155,
    202, 208, 239, 295, 302, 335, 340, 351,
    355, 367, 383, 387, 409, 419, 434, 448,
    453, 483, 487, 488, 495, 514, 529, 547,
    627, 670, 678, 786
JUSTICE(S) (*SEE* JUDGES(S))   134,
    148, 153, 155, 158, 159, 166, 167, 176,
    179, 180, 187, 191, 217, 225, 243, 272,
    292, 299, 351, 362, 385, 392, 425, 441,
    455, 457, 461, 463, 465, 474, 494, 515,
    520, 542, 547, 574, 576, 587, 592, 615,
    617, 644, 661, 692, 694, 705, 708, 721,
    722, 762, 766, 785, 788, 806, 808, 817,
    825, 829, 831, 835
JUSTICE WITH SEVERITY   59
JUSTIFICATION   47
JUSTIFYING GRACE   63
JUSTINIAN   266
JUSTINIANO   257, 560
JUSTINIUS   807

LOGIRE   206
LOLLARD(S)   456
LOLLIA   277, 554
LOLLIO   712, 717, 810
LOMBARDY/LOMBARD(S)   333,
   422, 624, 654
LOMIA   69
LONDON   87, 93, 96, 114, 119, 142,
   148, 153, 155, 175, 208, 212, 215, 224,
   233, 295, 302, 311, 322, 332, 335, 338,
   351, 399, 400, 409, 419, 448, 451, 460,
   466, 495, 566, 635, 676, 678.5, 826
LONDONER(S)   85, 93, 175, 176,
   182, 187, 214, 217, 222, 242, 244, 247,
   250, 251, 255, 257, 262, 263, 266, 276,
   292, 298, 299, 303, 304, 316, 323, 330,
   333, 334, 336, 352, 356, 425, 433, 442,
   445, 451, 455, 456, 457, 460, 461, 462,
   463, 473, 476, 477, 481, 507, 509, 517,
   518, 521, 523, 531, 535, 540, 542, 549,
   558, 563, 568, 574, 576, 586, 587, 591,
   592, 594, 606, 616, 617, 635, 644, 666,
   679, 691, 693, 699, 702, 711, 718, 720,
   721, 722, 739, 770, 771, 773, 778, 788,
   799, 801, 806, 808, 809, 817, 821, 829
LONEY   182
LONG   298
LONG MEG   411, 585
LONGAVILLE   150, 162, 641, 662,
   670
LONGFIELD   323
LONGING FOR COMFORT   64
LONGINO   724
LONGINUS   296
LONGSHANKS   112, 520
LONG-TONGUE   510
LONGUEVILLE   641, 662
LONG-VACATION   473
LOPEZ   127, 490, 638, 658, 664
LORD ADMIRAL   451, 835
LORD CHAMBERLAIN   104, 129,
   142, 197, 215, 224, 400, 491, 585, 689,
   835
LORD CHANCELLOR   215, 400,
   550, 835
LORD CHIEF JUSTICE   148, 155,
   167, 351, 835
LORD CONTROLLER   689, 835
LORD HIGH ADMIRAL   133, 451,
   835

LORD HIGH CONSTABLE   148,
   237, 400, 490, 550, 835
LORD HIGH MARSHAL   109, 141,
   400, 516, 597, 810, 835
LORD HIGH STEWARD   400, 835
LORD KEEPER OF THE SEAL   585
LORD MAYOR OF LONDON   96,
   114, 142, 148, 153, 155, 175, 212, 215,
   224, 295, 322, 335, 351, 399, 400, 409,
   460, 495, 815
LORD PRIVY SEAL   585, 835
LORD PROTECTOR   360, 386, 572,
   783
LORD STEWARD   585, 749
LORD TREASURER   114, 256, 550,
   585, 689, 835
LORD WARDEN   166, 510, 835
LORECE   771
LOREL   618
LORENZO   110, 172, 176, 221, 252,
   297, 306, 362, 498, 598, 601, 717, 729,
   758, 811, 816
LORETTA   362
LORRAINE   133, 140, 205, 729
LORRIQUE   438
LOTHAIRE   604
LOTHARIO   427, 471
LOTTI   508
LOUDEN   686
LOUIS (*SEE* LEWIS)   515, 717
LOUIS V OF FRANCE, THE MEEK
   162
LOUIS XI OF FRANCE   138, 154
LOUIS, DAUPHIN OF FRANCE
   101, 102, 165, 398
LOUIS OF FRANCE   210
LOVE   47, 64, 85, 92, 93, 104, 109,
   181, 202, 288, 311, 344, 351, 359, 434,
   483, 497, 500, 514, 546, 572, 582, 607,
   613, 686, 731, 738
LOVEALL   465, 829
LOVEGOOD   563
LOVELESS   334, 631
LOVELL   126, 142, 154, 175, 400,
   442, 474
LOVELY   718
LOVER(S)   16, 319, 437, 440, 502,
   508, 571, 713, 738, 777
LOVER AND BELOVED   16
LOVER NOT BELOVED   16

MAGPY   510
MAGUS   353
MAGUS(I)   118, 570
MAHARBALL   513
MAHOMATES   447
MAHOMET   127, 130, 156, 220, 447,
  489, 744, 793
MAIA   339
MAID MARIAN   158, 179, 180, 353,
  548, 618
MAID(S) OF HONOUR   366, 400,
  405, 436, 470, 480, 683, 688, 731, 732,
  749
MAILLARD   307
MAIMED SOLDIER(S)   493
MAINE   674.5
MAJESTY   202, 365
MAJOR   487, 692
MAJOR(S)   689
MAJORCA   215
MAKESHIFT   594
MALACIA   269
MALAENA   471
MALATESTA   418
MALATESTE   389, 490
MALBECCO   826
MALBY   258
MALCHUS   623
MALCOLM   404, 740
MALCONTENT(S) (SEE MELAN-
  CHOLIC(S))   100, 121, 149, 163,
  168, 185, 197, 203, 221, 246, 253, 306,
  379, 389, 394, 402, 418, 420, 427, 436,
  442, 461, 465, 479, 547, 549, 555, 620,
  735, 746, 777, 835
MALEFORT   559
MALEPERT   416
MALEVENTO   440
MALEVOLE   203
MALEVOLO   746
MALFA   689
MALFATO   555
MALFI   389
MALFORT   649
MALGO   229
MALHEUREUX   214
MALICE   30, 186, 280, 434, 489
MALICIOUS JUDGEMENT   47
MALIGNANT(S)   678.5
MALIGO   576

MALINDO   314
MALINGUA   361
MALIPIERO   747
MALL (SEE MOLL)   161, 177, 214,
  242, 336, 356, 494, 558, 574
MALLICORN   662
MALORY   632
MALOTIN   464
MALRODA   661
MALTA/MALTESE   109, 306, 388,
  409, 470, 475, 659, 760, 834
MALTHORA   701
MALUS GENIUS   514, 760
MALVEZZO   418
MALVOLIO   396
MAMILLIUS   397
MAMMON   303, 473, 631
MAMON   177
MAN   17, 18
MAN, ISLE OF   129
MANASSES   235, 710
MANCHESTER   113
MANDANE   360, 570
MANDEVILL   591, 806
MANDRECARD   123
MANDUBRATIUS   482
MANDUD   39
MANES   84
MANESIA   447
MANFREDY   254
MANFROY   758
MANHOOD   5, 38, 53, 76
MANHURST   509
MANIA   319
MANILIUS   605
MANLEY   692
MANLIUS   327, 620
MANLY   457, 477
MANNERING   158
MANNERS   459, 496
MANOPHES   567
MANSCOLD   586
MANSFIELD   274, 613
MANSIPULA   65
MANSIPULUS   65
MANSUETUDE   496, 500, 547, 634
MANTALDO   562
MANTESIO   314
MANTLE   179
MANTLE BARON(S)   112

MARTHESIA   671
MARTIA   75, 146, 159, 657, 705
MARTIAL   516
MARTIALIS   200
MARTIANO   774
MARTIANUS   229
MARTIN   192, 409, 475, 594, 617, 672, 673, 687, 708
MARTINE   653
MARTINES   440
MARTINO   205, 281, 555, 705, 758, 760
MARTINUS   224
MARTIO   602
MARTIUS   106, 117, 401, 670
MARTYRO   797
MARULLO   408
MARULLUS   403
MARWOOD   425
MARY   47, 112, 161, 191, 212, 214, 285, 298, 356, 396, 411, 433, 476, 507, 516, 546, 558, 579, 585, 788
MARY, QUEEN OF ENGLAND   215, 256
MASHAM   165
MASISTES   570
MASKER(S)   110, 143, 149, 150, 168, 172, 180, 181, 185, 188, 195, 203, 207, 211, 214, 230, 237, 238, 241, 247, 253, 266, 269, 270, 271, 275, 280, 283, 290, 291, 299, 301, 309, 310, 315, 318, 319, 320, 324, 327, 329, 343, 344, 345, 347, 348, 349, 350, 357, 358, 381, 382, 385, 389, 390, 394, 400, 402, 407, 411, 420, 429, 436, 437, 452, 453, 454, 458, 462, 463, 472, 478, 482, 486, 488, 491, 492, 496, 497, 498, 499, 502, 503, 508, 512, 524, 526, 527, 544, 545, 547, 549, 552, 556, 560, 562, 570, 571, 572, 578, 582, 583, 586, 592, 595, 599, 604, 606, 607, 610, 611, 617, 637, 645, 652, 653, 654, 665, 666, 680, 703, 707, 713, 727, 738, 746, 749, 759, 767, 771, 773, 780, 782, 788, 795, 796, 806, 807, 816, 823, 835
MASLIN   473
MASON   121
MASON(S) (*SEE* BRICKLAYER(S))   382, 736, 772
MASQUERADO   345
MASSAJETS   280

MASSANISSA   513
MASSENELLO   689
MASSINISSA   231
MASSINO   315
MASTER(S)   69, 118, 119, 120, 153, 157, 170, 197, 206, 218, 220, 260, 272, 295, 312, 317, 322, 332, 362, 389, 390, 409, 430, 435, 444, 456, 459, 488, 501, 502, 526, 527, 533, 549, 602, 618, 619, 630, 656, 657, 658, 669, 692, 721, 731, 732, 746, 760, 766, 779, 781, 792, 835
MASTER BEE   602
MASTER GUNNER(S)   355, 399, 739
MASTIFF(S)   686
MATCH   516
MATCHIL   809
MATE(S) (*SEE* SAILOR(S))   69, 119, 218, 322, 332, 355, 527, 739
MATER   37, 65
MATHEA   336
MATHEMATICIAN(S)   312, 616, 724
MATHEO   176, 204, 435
MATHETES   78
MATHIAS   436, 438, 475, 564
MATHO   384, 807
MATILDA   179, 180, 565, 749, 758, 784
MATREVIS   129
MATRON(S)   306, 354, 495, 578
MATT   336, 587
MATTALOONE   689
MATTEMORES   796
MATTHEW   46, 119, 153, 154, 176, 222
MATZAGENTE   184, 185
MATZED   744
MAUDLIN   395, 433, 492, 585, 591, 618, 809
MAUL   512, 614
MAURICE   788
MAURITANIA/MAURITANIAN(S)   445
MAURITIO   519
MAURON   327
MAURUCIO   478
MAVIS   304
MAVORTIUS   290
MAWD   494
MAWSY   494

MAWWORM   276
MAXIMILIAN   281
MAXIMINIAN   654
MAXIMINUS   380, 531
MAXIMUS   95, 240, 667
MAY   302, 339, 544
MAY DAY   358
MAY LADY(IES)   152, 309, 614
MAY LORD(S)   309, 614
MAY-BE-GOOD   56
MAYBERRY   250
MAYOR(S)   73, 74, 96, 107, 114, 119,
    129, 138, 142, 148, 153, 155, 166, 175,
    212, 215, 224, 295, 322, 335, 351, 399,
    400, 409, 445, 460, 487, 491, 495, 510,
    626, 688, 714, 740, 815
MAZARA   506
MAZARES   694
MAZERES   567
MEAGER   507
MEANDER   94, 497
MEANWELL   702, 806
MEASURE   11
MEASURER(S)   312
MEATH   472
MEATMAN(MEN)   580
MECHANIC ARTS   731, 732
MECHANICAL(S)   170, 290, 823
MECHANT   277
MEDEA   39, 44, 94, 136, 156, 313,
    332, 566, 675, 794
MEDESA   139
MEDIA   40, 94
MEDICE   226
MEDICI   139, 203, 275, 306, 796
MEDICO   431, 816
MEDICUS   135, 353
MEDINA   315, 386, 471, 804
MEDINA/MEDINAN(S)   221, 224,
    490, 598
MEDIOCRITY   69, 547
MEDLAR   802
MEDLAY   617
MEDLER   262
MEDOR   123
MEDORUS   325, 548
MEDULLA   441
MEDUSA   86
MEDWAY   291, 409
MEEKNESS   18, 162, 311, 367

MEERE-CRAFT   457
MEG   352, 411, 474, 494, 585, 748
MEGAERA (SEE FURIES)   29, 34,
    39, 104, 554, 673
MEGRA   363
MELA   578
MELAMPO   629
MELAMPUS   537
MELANCHOLIC(S) (SEE MAL-
    CONTENT(S))   82, 106, 107,
    109, 110, 117, 143, 144, 149, 150, 168,
    169, 172, 176, 177, 181, 203, 221, 225,
    230, 236, 239, 252, 253, 265, 272, 284,
    287, 299, 306, 386, 388, 389, 391, 402,
    411, 420, 423, 425, 429, 430, 436, 438,
    441, 442, 450, 465, 469, 474, 477, 480,
    482, 484, 492, 493, 499, 510, 513, 515,
    534, 536, 541, 548, 553, 557, 561, 564,
    573, 576, 582, 584, 586, 589, 590, 592,
    597, 618, 621, 641, 649, 652, 665, 681,
    719, 747, 752, 760, 773, 784, 785, 806,
    817, 833
MELANCHOLIC LOVER(S)   437
MELANCHOLICO   353, 746
MELANCHOLY   237, 514, 586, 767
MELANTIUS   357
MELARNUS   539
MELCOSHUS   780
MELEAGER   260, 313, 671
MELEANDER   420
MELEBEUS   105, 111, 227
MELEK   220
MELESIPPUS   735
MELETZA   252
MELIADUS   342
MELIBAEA   10, 439
MELICHUS   410
MELIDOR   621
MELIDORO   797
MELINDA   575
MELINTUS   620, 790
MELIPPUS   84
MELISSA   123, 537, 581, 738, 790
MELISSO   745
MELITUS   648
MELLACRITES   106
MELLIDA   184, 185
MELLIFLEUR   618
MELLISEUS   294
MELORA   684

611, 625, 626, 627, 629, 634, 653, 695,
731, 732, 734, 737, 738, 745, 754, 756,
768, 775, 782, 790, 800, 807, 835
NYMPHADORA   744
NYMPHADORO   230
OAF   441
OATCAKE   168
OATH   251
OBEDIENCE   64, 335, 409, 495
OBEDIENT GOODWILL   66
OBERON   149, 170, 343, 548, 602,
777, 818
OBLIGATION   465
OBLIVIO   202
OBLIVION   202, 208, 504, 527, 595
OBSCENE   776
OCCANON   88
OCCHIALI   130
OCCULTO   705
OCCUPATION   18
OCEAN   280
OCEANIAE   269
OCEANUS   98, 269, 366, 409, 421,
437, 466, 803
OCTA   822
OCTAVIA   45, 147, 405, 554
OCTAVIAN   232, 327, 715
OCTAVIANO   434
OCTAVIO   268, 305, 532, 538, 638,
758
OCTAVIUS   108, 122, 132, 147, 186,
403, 405, 698
OCYRHOE   269
OCYTE   269
ODILLIA   171
ODIRIS   541
ODMER   780
O'DORNEY   585
ODOUR   239
OECONOMA   353
OECONOMICUS   602
OEDIPUS   36, 61, 79, 450
OENEUS   313
OENONE   83, 467, 499, 756
OETES   313
OFFA   531, 772
OFFERING   606
OFFICER(S)   31, 53, 67, 68, 70, 73,
74, 84, 85, 93, 110, 117, 119, 136, 140,
141, 143, 145, 148, 150, 153, 154, 155,
163, 165, 166, 167, 172, 174, 175, 179,

182, 189, 191, 197, 204, 211, 214, 217,
220, 222, 229, 240, 242, 243, 244, 251,
253, 256, 258, 259, 265, 272, 275, 277,
290, 292, 293, 300, 303, 306, 315, 328,
333, 335, 352, 368, 379, 380, 382, 384,
386, 388, 389, 392, 393, 395, 396, 397,
398, 399, 400, 401, 402, 404, 405, 406,
408, 420, 425, 436, 440, 441, 442, 450,
451, 455, 457, 459, 461, 464, 469, 472,
475, 478, 479, 480, 486, 488, 491, 494,
501, 502, 509, 515, 517, 521, 523, 531,
533, 536, 542, 550, 553, 558, 559, 560,
565, 574, 577, 580, 582, 584, 586, 589,
590, 591, 592, 593, 598, 601, 605, 613,
617, 621, 636, 638, 640, 644, 645, 646,
649, 652, 653, 654, 655, 661, 662, 673,
684, 690, 692, 694, 697, 702, 704, 705,
714, 716, 719, 725, 726, 727, 733, 739,
741, 744, 747, 752, 757, 758, 766, 784,
785, 788, 789, 792, 793, 796, 801, 802,
815, 816, 823, 826, 832, 835
OGE   220
OGIER   123
O'HANLON   220
OLARI   834
OLAUS   752
OLD CHRISTMAS   606
OLD CLOTHES MAN(MEN)   643
OLD MEN/WOMEN (SEE SENEX)
OLDCASTLE   148, 166, 167
OLDCRAFT   666
OLDHAM   166
OLDRAT   521
OLDRENTS   708
OLDUNS   679
OLFACTUS   4, 202, 208, 239, 311,
335, 496, 514
OLINDA   443, 620, 649, 751
OLIVE   149, 236
OLIVER   123, 136, 176, 222, 249, 251,
272, 292, 394, 433, 455, 463, 465, 632,
672, 673, 680, 708, 718, 722, 778, 815,
823
OLIVIA   396, 725
OLOARITUS   554
OLWY   291
OLYMPA   744
OLYMPIA   95, 309, 408, 647, 828
OLYMPIAS   260, 357
OLYNDUS   701
OMAY   744

PANDION   82
PANDOLFO   330
PANDOLPH   749
PANDORA   144, 465
PANDORSUS   697
PANDULPH   101, 102, 398
PANDULPHO   185, 582, 657, 726,
   816
PANELION   99
PANGO   52
PANOPE   775
PANTALONI   719
PANTALOON(S)   120, 320, 607
PANTAMORA   797
PANTHEA   131, 360
PANTHINO   391
PANTILIUS   186, 195
PANTLER(S)   215, 565
PANTOFLE   286
PANURA   650
PAOLO   648
PAPHINITIUS   78
PAPHLAGONIA/PAPHLAGONIAN(S)
   118
PAPHOS   504, 637
PAPILLION   809
PAPLEWICK   618
PAQUETTO   60
PARACELSO   434
PARADINE   422
PARADO   555
PARASITE(S) (SEE CREATURE(S),
   FAVORITE(S), MINION(S))
   10, 31, 39, 46, 58, 60, 68, 69, 73, 74, 86,
   92, 115, 129, 135, 141, 149, 163, 175,
   176, 184, 186, 203, 216, 222, 229, 230,
   239, 259, 395, 402, 416, 428, 442, 461,
   463, 464, 484, 485, 498, 515, 519, 526,
   541, 551, 552, 554, 561, 562, 593, 616,
   617, 620, 657, 716, 720, 727, 730, 733,
   752, 807, 811
PARCAE   341, 350, 487
PARDONER(S)   14, 21, 194
PARENTHESIS   257
PARIDEL   241
PARIS   83, 143, 279, 424, 467, 468,
   499, 592, 627, 653, 695
PARIS/PARISIAN(S)   133, 159, 171,
   212, 399, 409, 639, 649, 662, 706, 770,
   809
PARISHIONER(S)   638

PARK KEEPER(S)   425, 517
PARLIAMENT   673.5, 674, 676, 677,
   678, 678.5
PARLIAMENT MAN(MEN)   366,
   602, 605, 680, 701, 835
PARMA/PARMAN(S)   486, 493, 536,
   577, 684, 724, 758
PARMENIO   84, 196, 811
PARMENO   10, 416, 439
PARNELL   494, 617, 757, 818
PAROLLES   395
PAROMET   761
PARR   212
PARRY   224
PARSIMONIOUS   602
PARSIMONY   434
PARSON(S)   14, 85, 114, 150, 166,
   187, 193, 194, 225, 299, 303, 304, 321,
   337, 356, 384, 396, 426, 433, 463, 474,
   591, 616, 658, 693, 699, 711, 808, 820,
   826, 829
PARTHENIA   557, 766, 790
PARTHENIUS   424
PARTHENOPE   448
PARTHENOPHIL   241, 420
PARTHESIA/PARTHESIAN(S)   556
PARTHIA/PARTHIAN(S)   94, 387,
   405
PARTIALITY   40, 434
PARTNER(S)   740
PARUM   547
PARVAGRACIO   361
PAS   443
PASIAS   743
PASIBULA   415
PASITHAS   541
PASQUIL   177, 354
PASSARELLO   203, 519
PASSENGER(S)   455, 669
PASSION   595
PASSIONATE BEE   602
PASSIONATE LORD(S)   652
PASSIONS   613, 746
PASTIME   53
PASTIMES   835
PASTOR(S)   303
PASTORALIS   602
PASYPHILO   60
PAT   149
PATACION   703
PATCH   212

PENSIONER(S)　　　215, 241, 835
PENTAPOLIS　　284
PENTHEA　　480
PENTHESILEA　　280, 468
PENULO　　92
PENURIO　　664
PENURY　　93, 547, 788
PEOPLE (*SEE* RABBLE)　　53, 537, 605
PEPPE　　689
PEPPERTON　　778
PERCIVALL　　126, 673
PERCO　　794
PERCY　　102, 140, 141, 145, 149, 167, 520
PERDICAS　　95, 223, 260, 605
PERDITA　　397
PERDUES　　833
PERECELL　　451
PEREGRINE　　259, 451, 521, 586
PERENOTTO　　479
PEREZ　　598
PERFECT　　356
PERFECT LOVE　　311
PERFECTIO　　270
PERFECTION　　351
PERFIDIOUS　　666
PERFUMER(S)　　262, 464, 724
PERICLES　　284
PERICOT　　307
PERIDOR　　628
PERIDURE　　229
PERIGOT　　287
PERILINDA　　730
PERILLUS　　213, 314
PERIM　　84
PERIN　　115
PERINDO　　745
PERINDUS　　443
PERIPHERE　　269
PERITHOUS　　317, 835
PERIWIGMAKER(S)　　293
PERIWINKLE　　263
PERJURER(S)　　468, 810
PERJURUS　　709
PERJURY　　680
PERKIN　　491
PERO　　246
PEROLOT　　670
PERON　　689
PERORATOR(S)　　54

PERPETUAL FOREMAN OF THE GRAND INQUEST　　496
PERPETUANA　　290
PERPLEXITY　　40
PERPURGERUS　　791
PERSEDA　　109, 110
PERSEUS　　136, 280, 317, 466, 569
PERSEVERANCE　　3, 5, 11
PERSIA/PERSIAN(S)　　40, 56, 94, 95, 131, 149, 196, 209, 223, 248, 278, 324, 333, 408, 421, 447, 497, 541, 569, 570, 584, 622, 654, 719, 744, 746, 800
PERSINA　　584
PERSIPHONE　　823
PERSPICE　　522
PERSUASION　　52, 66, 346
PERT　　507
PERTENAX　　690
PERTILLO　　182
PERTINAX　　303, 387
PERU/PERUVIAN(S)　　787, 798
PERVERSE DOCTRINE　　58
PESCARA　　386, 389
PESTIFERO　　361
PETARRE　　523
PETELLA　　706
PETER　　63, 85, 105, 119, 120, 126, 143, 167, 170, 189, 195, 210, 234, 251, 263, 264, 281, 321, 381, 392, 579, 642, 646, 659, 823
PETER OF GALILEE　　579
PETER OF POMFRET　　101, 102, 398
PETER THE HERMIT　　329
PETERS　　680, 688
PETESCA　　647
PETILLIUS　　655
PETITIONER(S) (*SEE* SUITOR(S))　　15, 119, 171, 418, 434, 435, 445, 453, 459, 460, 472, 538, 541, 550, 559, 567, 570, 595, 654, 714, 724, 733, 752, 759, 796, 807, 810, 815, 834
PETO　　145, 167, 176
PETOUNE　　255
PETRAEA　　269, 504
PETREIUS　　296
PETRO　　446, 601
PETROCELLA　　509
PETRONEL　　217
PETRONELLA　　505
PETRONIO　　726
PETRONIUS　　410, 554, 660

PETRUCHI   716
PETRUCHIO   60, 120, 143, 478, 498,
   505, 582, 601, 646, 660, 810, 811
PETTIFOG   817
PETTY PORT   835
PETTYFOGGER(S)   227, 365
PETULA   195
PETULIUS   178
PETULUS   106
PEWTERER(S)   148, 316
PEYTON   674.5
PHAEDRA   80, 696
PHAEDRIA   416
PHAENICIA   569
PHALLAX   73, 74
PHANATICUS   709
PHANCY   746
PHANTASM(S)   473, 607
PHANTASMA   225
PHANTASTE   181, 527
PHANTASTES   239, 353, 836
PHANTASTIC LOVER(S)   437
PHANTASTICO   361
PHANTASY   607
PHAO   82
PHARAMOND   363
PHARETES   675
PHARISEE(S)   24, 47, 623
PHARMACOPLIS   602
PHAROAH   710
PHASIACA   146
PHASIS   313
PHEANDER   327, 819
PHEBE (*SEE* PHOEBE)   394, 595,
   651
PHEGO   286
PHEME   218
PHEMILIA   628
PHEMIS   310
PHEMONE   580
PHEROAS   382
PHERORAS   308
PHEUDIPPE   314
PHIB   718
PHIDIAS   667
PHIDIPPIDES   743
PHIL   701, 720, 739
PHILAEMA   241
PHILAENIS   701
PHILAGRIO   742

PHILALETHES   614
PHILAN   541
PHILANAX   235, 459
PHILANDER   39, 164, 648, 694, 738,
   771
PHILANT   750
PHILANTHUS   779
PHILARCHUS   115, 290, 557, 715
PHILARGUS   424, 807
PHILARIO   406
PHILARITUS   761
PHILARMONUS   406
PHILASTER   363
PHILASTRUS   260
PHILATEL   628
PHILAUTIA   181
PHILAUTUS   69, 283, 461
PHILEMA   120, 480
PHILEMON   284, 620
PHILEMUS   94
PHILENA   120, 738
PHILENZO   286, 479
PHILERNO   199
PHILICIA   551, 552
PHILINAX   459
PHILIP   50, 101, 102, 116, 120, 139,
   140, 148, 161, 236, 250, 257, 302, 332,
   360, 398, 409, 442, 463, 550, 739, 777,
   778, 809, 818
PHILIP II OF FRANCE   398
PHILIP II OF SPAIN   215, 220, 582,
   777
PHILIP, DAUPHIN OF FRANCE
   210
PHILIPPA   140, 582, 705
PHILIPPO   109, 254, 478, 508, 653,
   669, 777, 816
PHILISTUS   539, 694
PHILLIDA   105, 139, 534, 779
PHILLIP   821
PHILLIS   97, 242, 323, 325, 629, 695,
   698, 722, 745, 756, 806, 818, 825
PHILO   405, 743
PHILOBERTO   538
PHILOBLATHICI   808
PHILOCALIA   195, 230
PHILOCALUS   68
PHILOCLEA   583
PHILOCLES   277, 384, 572, 807
PHILOCTETES   81, 313, 317

PIEDMANTLE   456
PIEDMONT   684, 796
PIERCE   50, 141, 442
PIERO   184, 185, 253, 429, 470, 508,
    555, 599
PIERRE   154
PIERS   11, 115, 129, 141
PIETRO   203, 538, 575
PIETY   53, 55, 351, 387, 495, 546, 823
PIG   808
PIG(S)   454, 503
PIGEON(S)   117
PIGMY(IES)   453, 514, 608, 835
PIGOT   112
PIGWIDGIN   697
PIG-WOMAN(WOMEN)   455
PIKEMAN(MEN)   421
PILATE   579
PILCH   284
PILCHER   188
PILGRIM(S) (*SEE* PALMER(S))   21,
    63, 103, 156, 171, 213, 305, 381, 389,
    395, 409, 506, 567, 584, 658, 704, 736,
    772, 775, 797, 810, 819
PILIA-BORZA   475
PILOT(S)   483, 497
PILUMNUS   548
PIMME   672
PIMOS   74
PIMP(S) (*SEE* PANDAR(S))   428,
    474, 540, 773, 788, 808, 828
PIMPONIO   575
PIMPWELL   773
PINAC   706
PINCH   393
PINCKANIE   290
PINCKCARCASE   711
PINDARUS   403, 534
PINEDA   509
PINIERO   650
PINNACIA   442
PINNARIO   715
PINNARIUS   216, 553
PINNER(S)   158
PIONEER(S)   295
PIORATTO   204, 661
PIPEAU   565
PIPENETTA   106
PIPER(S)   234, 585
PIPEROLLO   724
PIPKIN   191

PIPPO   252
PIRACCO   833
PIRACQUO   712, 728
PIRAMONT   628
PIRATE(S)   69, 119, 284, 300, 306,
    392, 405, 430, 559, 619, 620, 640, 656,
    657, 739, 760, 828
PIRITHOUS   492
PIRKE   594
PISA/PISAN(S)   120, 508, 601, 833
PISANDER   408, 600
PISANIO   406
PISANO   127, 498, 758
PISARO   336
PISAURO   575
PISCES   271, 367, 496, 595, 778
PISISTRATUS   735
PISO   176, 240, 255, 410, 642, 698, 719
PISSE-BREECH   188
PISTOCLERUS   671
PISTOL   165, 167, 187
PISTON   109, 513
PISTOPHOENAX   227
PIT-FALL   457
PITHIAS   58, 416, 455
PITHO   626
PITIFUL PARLIAMENT   674
PITS   356
PITY   3, 434
PIUS   117
PLACEBO   193, 194
PLACENTA   465
PLACENTIA   616, 727
PLACIBILITY   500
PLACILLA   807
PLACKET   263
PLAGUE(S)   57
PLAIN AND JUST   64
PLAIN HELP   70
PLAINE-DEALING   241
PLAINTIFF(S)   365, 496, 796
PLANCUS   147, 553
PLANET   177
PLANETIUS   694
PLANETS   317, 487
PLANGUS   813
PLANTAGENET   101, 102, 119, 121,
    138, 140, 142, 165, 398, 399, 729, 749
PLASTER   576
PLASTERER(S)   614
PLATE-SELLER(S)   295

PROPERTY-MAN(MEN)   488
PROPHET(S) (*SEE* AUGUR(S),
   ORACLE(S),   SOOTHSAYER(S))
   22, 57, 72, 98, 101, 102, 118, 158, 160,
   183, 289, 398, 450, 467, 526, 554, 611,
   629, 650, 698, 708, 822
PROPHETESS(ES)   142, 279, 319,
   467, 468, 485, 654
PROPHILUS   480
PROPOSITION   556
PROREX   602
PROSAITES   181
PROSERPINA   207
PROSERPINE   317, 504
PROSPERITY   11, 30, 351, 566
PROSPERO   176, 388, 390, 668, 684,
   719, 736
PROSPICE   522
PROSTITUTE(S) (*SEE* COURTE-
   ZAN(S))   20, 31, 41, 47, 85, 93,
   153, 154, 166, 191, 217, 230, 243, 255,
   284, 293, 297, 306, 314, 323, 484, 574,
   640, 788
PROTALDIE   368
PROTEA   178
PROTECTOR(S)   119, 142, 286, 360,
   386, 399, 418, 459, 572, 777, 783, 801
PROTESTANT(S)   133
PROTEUS   357, 391, 407, 411, 437,
   546, 835
PROTHEUS   90
PROTHYMIA   200
PROTONOTARY OF ABUSES   496
PROUD   618
PROUD ASS   504
PROUD LOVER(S)   437
PROUDLY   356
PROVERBS   161
PROVIDENCE   157, 202, 208, 355,
   367, 383, 419
PROVIDENT LOVER(S)   437
PROVINCIAL   694
PROVISION   48, 78
PROVISOR(S)   389, 532
PROVOST(S)   156, 171, 216, 220, 295,
   392, 506, 639, 654
PROXIMUS   822
PRUDENCE   21.5, 47, 53, 181, 202,
   208, 298, 383, 442, 483, 495, 514, 585,
   786
PRUDENTIA   796

PRUDENTILLA   484
PRUDENTIUS   746
PRUE   585
PRUSIAS   286, 513, 703
PRUSSIA/PRUSSIAN(S)   438
PRYNNE   686
PSECTAS   384
PSEUDODOCTRINA   24
PSORABEUS   301
PSYCHE   239, 504
PSYCHROTE   269
PSYL(S)   553
PSYLLUS   84
PSYTERIA   60
PTOLEMY   146, 260, 405, 645, 651
PUBLIUS   1, 2, 117, 122, 186, 273,
   296, 403, 453, 698
PUCELLE   399
PUCHANNELLO   796
PUCK   170, 618
PUCKLING   494
PUDD   794
PUDDING-LANE   606
PUDDLEDWARF   455
PUFF   177, 292
PUG   457
PUGILI   453
PULCHERIA   459, 724
PULCHRINA   626
PULSE-FEEL   721
PULTROT   652
PUMICESTONE   521
PUNCH   756
PUNK(S) (*SEE* WHORE(S))   455,
   597, 715, 808
PUNTARVOLO   163
PUNTO   428
PUNY   693, 802
PUPIL(S)   721
PUPILLUS   597
PUPPET(S)   455
PUPPETEER(S)   455
PUPPY   455, 585, 617
PURBECK   585
PURE ADORATION   496
PURE ARTS   353
PURE ZEAL   93
PURECRAFT   455
PURGATO   361
PURGE   263
PURITAN(S)   59, 115, 134, 159, 162,

RAGAZZONI   241
RAGE   280
RAGOZINE   392
RAGUELIN   621
RAIGNSBOROUGH   673, 680
RAILER(S)   467, 468
RAIN   452
RAINBORNE   818
RAINBOW   549
RAINSBROUGH   687
RAINSFORD   739
RAKER(S)   748
RALPH (*SEE* RAFE, RAPHE)   1, 46,
    50, 153, 167, 179, 189, 205, 242, 264,
    272, 276, 298, 425, 515, 531, 542, 563,
    674, 679, 693, 749, 806, 808, 821, 826
RAM(S)   503, 806, 816
RAM ALLEY   292, 456
RAMBLE   788
RAMBURES   165
RAMIA   105
RAMIRES   723
RAMIS   178
RAMME   605
RAMPINO   624
RAMSES   710
RAMSEY   224
RAMUS   133
RANDALL   225, 476, 708, 740
RANDOLFO   252
RANDOLPH   699, 740
RANDULPHO   670
RANGER(S)   15, 164, 365, 455, 613,
    835
RANGINO   724
RANGONE   624
RANNIUS   405
RANOFF   364
RANOLA   833
RANTER(S)   697
RAPAX   73, 74
RAPE   117
RAPHAEL   63, 720
RAPHE (*SEE* RAFE, RALPH)   124,
    161, 169, 222, 264, 531
RAPIER   298, 331
RAPINE   349
RAPINUS   569
RAPTURE   521
RASH   323, 632
RASHBE   576

RASHLEY   806
RASI-CLENCH   617
RASIS   617
RASNI   118
RASTROSICO   719
RAT   67, 411
RATCLIFFE   142, 785
RATIONAL LOVER(S)   437
RATSBANE   327
RAVACK   620
RAVEN   576
RAVENSHAW   251
RAVILLAC   305
RAWBONE   425
RAYBRIGHT   767
RAYES   127
RAYMOND   205, 264, 300, 364, 582,
    656, 817
RAYNSFOORTH   739
RAYNULPH   815
RAYSBY   323
READER(S)   835
READY WIT   57
REAPER(S) (*SEE* HARVEST-
    MAN(MEN))   173, 365, 390
REARAGE   244
REASON   11, 17, 18, 52, 55, 57, 191,
    237, 489
REASONABLENESS   64
REBECCA   51, 263, 321, 587
REBECK   143
REBEL(S)   114, 119, 129, 145, 153,
    158, 166, 167, 434, 526, 583, 621, 740,
    741, 749, 752, 815
REBELLION   630, 631, 674
REBUS   301
RECONCILER(S)   618
RECORD   495
RECORDER(S)   153, 202, 225, 362,
    626, 636, 746, 767, 835
RECREATION   55
RED HOOD   613
RED STARCH   365
REDCAP   174
REDESDALE   149
REDRESS   11
REDUCTION   556
REEDE   107
REES AP VAUGHAN   195
REESE   609
REFINER(S)   295

RIGHT BATTING BAND   332
RIGHT GOVERNMENT   526
RIGOUR   43, 434
RIMEWELL   702
RINALDO   206, 219, 395, 670
RINATUS   813
RINGER(S)   574
RINGWOOD   688
RIOT   14.5, 20, 76, 302
RIOTER(S)   484, 508
RIOTOSSA   434
RIOVA   307
RIPPON   456
RISCIO   125
RISUS   271
RIVAL BEE   602
RIVER(S)   87, 200, 202, 208, 218, 270, 287, 288, 291, 332, 338, 409, 419, 452, 483, 487, 495, 496, 528, 529, 566, 629, 649, 731, 732, 835
RIVERS   126, 138, 142, 773
RIVIERO   538
RIXULA   125
RIXUS   152
ROARER(S) (*SEE* HECTORS(S))
        298, 303, 320, 323, 352, 356, 363, 434, 435, 441, 446, 455, 562, 571, 576, 601, 617, 646, 702, 747, 755, 769, 785, 788, 808, 831
ROBERT   101, 110, 112, 113, 126, 140, 142, 153, 154, 167, 174, 179, 180, 182, 187, 194, 248, 256, 285, 329, 332, 333, 337, 383, 398, 460, 465, 491, 494, 632, 702, 801, 826
ROBERTO   315, 470, 747
ROBIN   105, 119, 148, 166, 187, 205, 249, 337, 460, 465, 484, 494, 535, 540, 558, 606, 642, 662, 693, 749
ROBIN GOODFELLOW   153, 170, 234, 345, 527, 618, 826
ROBIN HOOD   32, 158, 174, 179, 180, 332, 618
ROBINHOOD-MAN(MEN)   318
ROBON   818
ROBUSTIO   697
ROCCA   659
ROCHELLE   171
ROCHESTER   114, 125, 155, 166, 302, 400
ROCHETTE   274

ROCHFIELD   817
ROCHFORT   464
ROCILIA   113
ROCK   732
RODAMANT   593
RODAMONT   123
RODER   258
RODERICK   531
RODERICO   478
RODERIGO   151, 254, 379, 389, 396, 434, 470, 471, 490, 525, 596, 605, 658, 669, 717, 723, 728, 777
RODERIGUE   236
RODERIGUEZ   707
RODERIQUE   471
RODIA   537
RODON   132
RODORICK   210, 438
RODORIGO   438
RODRIGUEZ   725
RODS-IN-PISS   358
ROE   686
ROGASTUS   709
ROGAT   715
ROGER   119, 129, 155, 166, 175, 176, 204, 214, 258, 334, 460, 484, 542, 561, 563, 585, 589, 626, 644, 679
ROGERO   221, 315, 397, 498, 727
ROGUE(S)   353, 397, 565, 699
ROHON   818
ROISEAU   274
ROISTER   50
ROISTER DOISTER   46
ROISTERER(S)   68
ROLANDO   668
ROLFO   604
ROLLANO   482
ROLLIARDO   479
ROLLO   565
ROLLS, MASTER OF THE   835
ROMAN(S)   1, 2, 14, 45, 65, 93, 108, 116, 117, 122, 132, 147, 186, 216, 231, 232, 240, 254, 261, 273, 283, 296, 327, 380, 382, 388, 389, 401, 403, 405, 406, 410, 419, 424, 444, 459, 482, 486, 488, 513, 531, 538, 545, 553, 554, 560, 578, 579, 640, 645, 654, 655, 667, 670, 698, 719, 733, 753, 765, 819, 823, 828
ROMANELLO   532
ROMANTIC LOVER(S)   437

ROMASTIGO 434

ROMBELO 151

ROMBUS 152

ROME 116, 117, 132, 186, 216, 273, 283, 296, 327, 365, 380, 382, 403, 405, 409, 410, 424, 444, 447, 531, 554, 578, 645, 654, 667, 698, 699, 733, 765, 823

ROMELIO 388

ROMEO 143

ROMERAKER 194

ROMERO 192, 797

ROMNEY 400

ROMONT 464

RONALDO 833

RONCA 330

RONCAS 274

RONVERE 657

ROOKESBY 212

ROOKSBILL 808

ROPUS 241

ROSABELLA 747

ROSALIND 394

ROSALINE 150, 184

ROSALURA 706

ROSALURE 706

ROSAMOND 298, 549

ROSANIA 725, 774

ROSARA 509

ROSAURA 727

ROSCIO 384

ROSCIUS 547

ROSE 175, 256, 456

ROSECLAP 568

ROSEILLI 478

ROSELLA 506

ROSELLIA 656

ROSENCRANTZ 197

ROSENCROFT 197

ROSIA 690

ROSILIO 113

ROSILION 123

ROSIN 617

ROSINDA 519, 771

ROSKO 73, 74

ROSS 141, 149, 404

ROSSA 278, 428

ROSSANA 657

ROSSILL 145, 167

ROSSILLION 395

ROSTEN 278

ROTERDAMUS 451

ROTHER 291

ROTHERHAM 142

ROTSIE 254

ROUEN 224, 782

ROUGECROSSE 520

ROUGHMAN 445, 446

ROUND-HEAD(S) 630, 680

ROUNDNESS 269

ROUSARD 293

ROUSE 798

ROUSILLON 395

ROWER(S) 495

ROWING 322

ROWKE 73

ROWLAND 175, 224, 392, 414, 589, 606, 644, 660, 785

ROWLE 159

ROXANE 88, 260, 671

ROXENA 815

ROXOLANA 763, 827

ROXONA 567

ROYAL VIRTUES 332

ROYALIST(S) 673

ROYALL 409

ROYALTY 194

RU 124

RUBBISH 414

RUBEN 300

RUBIN 127

RUBIO 707

RUDE 618

RUDESBY 228

RUDHUDIBRAS 616

RUDINGTON 510

RUDSTONE 256

RUFALDO 441

RUFF 56, 326

RUFFEL 255

RUFFETING(S) 290

RUFFIAN(S) 56, 59, 72, 85, 107, 118, 179, 182, 206, 222, 254, 411, 439, 444, 578, 582, 630, 639, 663, 714

RUFFIANO 835

RUFFLICT 721

RUFFORD 153, 154

RUFMAN 305

RUFUS 186, 195, 216, 554, 626

RUGBY 187

RUGECROSSE 520

RUGGLES   748

RUGIO   664, 665, 810

RUGWEED   802

RUIN   290

RUINA   124

RUINOUS   666

RULE   496

RUMMING   411

RUMOR   52, 65, 157, 167, 288, 324

RUNLET   507

RUNNAGADO(ES)   802

RUNNER(S)   517

RURIUS   761

RUSEE   565

RUSH   305

RUSHMAID(S)   226

RUSHMAN(MEN)   226

RUSSEE   565

RUSSELL   145, 167, 302, 352

RUSSET HOOD   613

RUSSETING(S)   290

RUSSIA/RUSSIAN(S) (*SEE*
     MOSCOVIA)   150, 224, 248, 333,
     351, 397, 419, 647, 835

RUSTAN   763, 827

RUSTIC(S) (*SEE* COUNTRYMAN
     (MEN))   121, 136, 163, 327, 361,
     366, 394, 425, 427, 463, 465, 471, 493,
     494, 505, 517, 542, 545, 547, 548, 583,
     587, 605, 617, 618, 664, 699, 759, 772,
     784, 796, 807, 810

RUSTICANUS   835

RUSTICITY   434

RUSTICO   361

RUSTICUS   48, 424

RUT   616

RUTH   214, 688

RUTILIO   640

RUTLAND   138, 141, 585

RUTULLUS   531

RUY DIAS   650

RYMBOMBO   443

RYVIERS   451

SAAVEDRA   661

SABA   569

SABELLI   590

SABIA   69

SABINA   410, 589, 765

SABINUS   216, 240

SABREN   136

SABRINA   524, 628, 765

SACERDOS   61, 314

SACKBURY   681

SACKVILLE   512

SACRAPANT   137

SACREPANT   123

SACRIFICER(S)   453, 738

SACRILEGE   465, 680

SAD   618

SAD CIRCUMSPECTION   11

SADD   829

SADLER   119, 189

SADNESS   11, 434

SADOC   160

SAFETY   200, 202, 208

SAGANA   485

SAGE(S)   59, 93, 118, 319, 618

SAGER   337

SAGITTARIUS   271, 367, 496, 500,
     595, 778

SAGO   315

SAILOR(S) (*SEE* MARINER(S),
     MATE(S))   3, 46, 69, 87, 93, 107,
     112, 118, 119, 127, 128, 135, 184, 197,
     217, 236, 241, 248, 284, 285, 290, 300,
     379, 396, 407, 430, 444, 445, 446, 482,
     484, 488, 495, 497, 501, 526, 537, 546,
     558, 568, 586, 619, 640, 643, 656, 657,
     659, 668, 673, 697, 739, 751, 757, 760,
     787, 792, 798, 817, 831

SAINT ALBANS   119, 166

SAINT ANDREW   202, 282, 545

SAINT ANDREW'S   149, 835

SAINT ANNE   236

SAINT ANTHONY   545

SAINT ANTLINGS   251

SAINT ASAPH   400

SAINT BARTHOLOMEWES   302

SAINT BENEDICT   429

SAINT CLARE   388

SAINT DAVID   545

SAINT DENIS   545

SAINT DUNSTAN   826

SAINT GEORGE   202, 282, 288, 496,
     545

SAINT GILES   835

SAINT HUGH   531

SAINT IAGO   248

SAINT JACQUES   475

SAINT JAMES   365, 545

SAINT JOHN THE BAPTIST   409
SAINT JOHN THE EVANGELIST
    26
SAINT JOHN OF JERUSALEM   409
SAINT KATHERINE   153, 366, 448,
    466, 522, 558
SAINT MARY OVERIES   251, 302
SAINT MICHAEL   306
SAINT NIHIL   85
SAINT PATRICK   545, 593
SAINT PAUL   63
SAINT PAUL'S   224
SAINT PETER   63, 579
SAINT PETER AD VINCULA   254
SAINT PIERRE   154
SAINT SWITHINS   740
SAINT TRINITY   302
SALADINE   834
SALADINO   434
SALAMANCA/SALAMANCAN(S)
    777
SALAMINE   313, 467
SALANIO   172
SALAPIA/SALAPIAN(S)   513
SALARINO   172
SALASSA   716
SALERIO   172
SALERNE   104
SALEWARE   718
SALEWIT   568
SALEWOOD   244
SALIBRAND   802
SALISBURY   101, 102, 114, 119, 129,
    140, 141, 142, 165, 179, 180, 212, 398,
    399
SALOME   308, 623
SALOMON   160
SALTATOR(S)   453
SALTERMAN(MEN)   182
SALTERS' COMPANY   302, 332,
    466
SALUCIA   52, 198
SALUMITH   382
SALUTATION   66
SALUZZO   52
SALVIUS   444, 698
SAM   262, 272, 433, 540, 558, 587
SAMATHIS   146
SAMIA   118
SAMIAS   99

SAMIUS   522
SAMLES   149
SAMORAT   628
SAMPSON   143, 639
SAMSON   589
SAMUEL   272, 558, 587
SANAZARRO   505
SANCHIO   598, 669, 816
SANCHO   525, 577, 596, 717
SANCTA CABRADO   362
SANCTO   192, 220
SANDANIS   209
SANDER   119, 120, 476
SANDERS   155
SANDFIELD   778
SANDS   400, 451
SANDWICH   153, 400
SANDY   193, 258
SANDYS   400
SANGA   296, 416
SANGO   560
SANGUIS   353
SANITONELLA   388
SANMARTINO   588
SANQUINIUS   216
SANSEVERIN   418
SANSFOY   157
SAPHIRA   797
SAPHO   82, 497, 557
SAPIENCE   11, 49, 53, 193
SAPRITIUS   380
SARA   71, 569
SARACEN(S)   445, 526
SARDINIA/SARDINIAN(S)   215,
    619
SARDIS   570
SARE   300
SARGUS   636
SARLOIS   438
SARON   407, 411
SARPEGO   226, 721
SARTANO   835
SARVIA   501
SASMENOS   458
SATAN   23, 41, 54, 57, 71, 72, 76.5,
    78, 115, 118, 254, 457
SATEROS   124
SATIETY   545
SATIRE   547
SATIRIST(S)   427

SATRIUS   216
SATURN   83, 92, 144, 294, 317, 319,
    385, 387, 454, 487, 571, 593, 595, 796
SATURNINE   117
SATURNINUS   117
SATYR(S)   97, 123, 162, 173, 183, 187,
    201, 234, 235, 287, 294, 320, 321, 324,
    339, 343, 385, 397, 417, 429, 441, 452,
    453, 454, 487, 488, 497, 527, 544, 549,
    600, 604, 629, 713, 734, 737, 756, 761,
    764, 768, 775, 795, 812
SATYRANE   241
SAUFELLUS   578
SAUNDER   476, 821
SAUNDERS   120
SAVAGE(S) (*SEE* WILD MAN(MEN))
    90, 390, 731, 732
SAVEALL   718
SAVELLI   532
SAVERNE   218
SAVIL   334
SAVIOLINA   163
SAVONA/SAVONESE   555
SAVOURWIT   778
SAVOY   138, 274, 306, 329, 429, 684,
    706, 796
SAWEN   487
SAWGUT   785
SAWYER   785
SAXON(S)   551, 552, 772, 815, 822
SAXON WAYMAR   564
SAXONY   89, 113, 115, 121, 169, 205,
    329, 364, 438, 472, 729, 772
SAY   119
SAY AND SEAL   677
SAY-MASTER(S)   295
SBIRRI   86
SCALES   119, 142, 154
SCANFARDO   362
SCANIA   604
SCAPETHRIFT   67, 217
SCAPHA   484
SCAPULA   327
SCARABEO   562
SCARBOROW   249
SCARCROW   831
SCAREFOOL   711
SCARLET   158, 179, 180, 242, 618
SCARPUS   553
SCARUS   405

SCATHLOCK   179, 180, 332, 618
SCATTERGOOD   323, 802
SCEDASUS   703
SCENAESE   60
SCENTLOVE   518
SCEROPES   421
SCEVA   645
SCEVINUS   410
SCEVOLA   273
SCHAHIN   458
SCHISM   676, 677
SCHISMATIC   586
SCHOLAR(S)   68, 72, 82, 121, 124,
    159, 163, 193, 194, 197, 198, 205, 225,
    234, 235, 241, 246, 247, 251, 252, 262,
    264, 290, 305, 311, 364, 365, 384, 389,
    409, 414, 420, 431, 435, 436, 442, 458,
    465, 472, 473, 480, 495, 515, 535, 547,
    555, 586, 591, 592, 601, 616, 658, 666,
    681, 697, 698, 706, 724, 743, 776, 778,
    806, 807, 809, 832, 836
SCHOOLBOY(S)   155, 252, 414, 810,
    836
SCHOOLGIRL(S)   810
SCHOOLMAN(MEN)   319
SCHOOLMASTER(S) (*SEE*
    TEACHER(S))
    68, 86, 133, 150, 152, 191, 206, 252, 257,
    336, 353, 385, 393, 405, 441, 492, 535,
    565, 613, 668, 721, 809, 836
SCHOOLMISTRESS(ES)   206, 568,
    810
SCIARRHA   498
SCIENCE   55, 72, 87, 526
SCIENCE AND LABOUR   96
SCIENCES   208, 302, 322, 421
SCILLA   122
SCILLICET   283
SCILLIE   285
SCINTILLA   99
SCIOLTO   428, 506
SCIPIO   122, 231, 513, 835
SCLAVONIAN(S)   719
SCOGAN   411
SCOLDER(S)   362
SCOLOPENDRA   536
SCONCE   594
SCOPAS   414
SCOPERTA   428
SCORN   349

SHOPKEEPER(S)   182, 702
SHORE   126, 153, 154
SHORT-HAND   679
SHORTHEELS   476
SHORTHOSE   195, 563, 826
SHORTTOOL   802
SHORTYARD   244
SHOW   431
SHREWD WIT   27
SHREWSBURY   399
SHRIMP   263
SHROVETIDE   543
SHROVE-TUESDAY   358
SHRUB   627
SHUNFIELD   456
SHYLOCK   172
SIB   821
SIBERT   824
SIBYL(S)   111, 488, 761
SICANIO   774
SICILUS   406
SICILY/SICILIAN(S)   60, 215, 277,
      297, 333, 362, 363, 384, 397, 443, 444,
      470, 506, 519, 539, 548, 588, 597, 599,
      619, 620, 694, 704, 724, 741, 760, 763,
      774, 792, 810, 811, 819, 827, 828
SICINIUS   401
SICKNESS   290, 545, 566
SICOPHANT(S)   229
SICOPHANTUS   805
SIDEROS   355
SIDNEY   332, 409
SIENNA/SIENNESE   60, 427, 470,
      532, 664, 796
SIGERUS   424
SIGHING   434
SIGHT   4, 202, 208, 239, 311, 335, 496,
      514, 522
SIGISMOND   95, 621, 741
SIJEIUS   424
SILENA   125
SILENCE   167, 527, 595
SILENI   734
SILENUS   320, 343, 487, 741
SILIUS   216, 405, 578
SILKMAN(MEN)   718
SILKWORM   616
SILLEUS   308, 741
SILLIO   811
SILLY   442

SILVER   208, 390
SILVER AGE   355
SILVESTRIS   178
SILVIA (*SEE* SYLVIA)   227, 325,
      391, 436, 532, 629
SILVIO   164, 183, 389, 536, 599, 629,
      644, 664, 705, 742
SIM   46, 244, 476
SIMANTHES   730
SIMATIO   416
SIMEON   710, 823
SIMKIN   11, 755
SIMNEL   121, 491
SIMO   12, 91, 415, 469
SIMON   47, 120, 137, 143, 167, 175,
      179, 251, 323, 702, 757, 815
SIMONIDES   284, 766, 815
SIMONY   25, 85, 93
SIMPATHUS   583
SIMPCOX   119
SIMPER   15
SIMPERINA   188
SIMPHOROSA   538
SIMPLE   187, 462
SIMPLETON   692, 769, 802
SIMPLICITY   59, 64, 85, 93, 181, 311,
      365, 670
SIMPLICIUS   252
SIMPLICUS   431
SIMPLO   361
SIMS   433
SIMULATION   43
SIN   47, 72
SINAM   130
SINATUS   551, 552
SINCERE DOCTRINE   59
SINCERITY   85, 93, 367, 500
SINDEFY   217
SINEVERO   783
SINEZI   204
SINGER(S)   20, 33, 55, 74, 84, 168,
      228, 233, 237, 238, 280, 290, 311, 316,
      320, 392, 394, 418, 420, 427, 428, 455,
      456, 465, 480, 488, 492, 499, 526, 541,
      568, 570, 606, 614, 622, 638, 643, 650,
      652, 653, 670, 681, 684, 690, 703, 721,
      726, 746, 759, 770, 803, 806, 811, 813,
      834
SINGING MASTER(S)   779, 781
SINKLO   203

SINQUAPACE   781
SINS   205
SIPARIUS   802
SIREN(S)   178, 407, 414, 448, 514, 731, 732, 803
SIRENO   745
SIS   516, 531, 606
SISAMNES   56
SISARMES   570
SISIGAMBIS   196
SISLEY   531
SISLY   258
SISMUND   300
SISTER(S)   652
SISTERUS   791
SIWARD   404
SIXTUS V   306
SIZAR(S)   121
SKALES   561
SKALLIGER   213
SKELTON   179, 180, 411
SKETON   491
SKILL   11, 93, 720
SKIMEON   823
SKIMINGTON   494
SKINK   174
SKINNERS' COMPANY   302, 332, 466
SKIPKENNEL   722
SKIPPER(S) (*SEE* CAPTAIN(S))
        111, 175, 202, 320, 324, 419, 497, 803, 831
SKIPPON   687
SKIRMISH   251
SLACK   247
SLANDER   237, 280, 349
SLAUGHTER   230
SLAVE(S)   61, 122, 125, 160, 231, 239, 300, 310, 380, 382, 390, 393, 408, 424, 458, 459, 475, 509, 533, 560, 570, 619, 620, 714, 733, 760, 780, 783, 798, 804, 816, 828, 834
SLAVE MASTER(S)   760
SLAVE MERCHANT(S)   760
SLAWTER   126
SLEDGE   457
SLEEP   207, 488, 527, 631, 776
SLEEPY   337
SLENDER   187
SLICER   702

SLIGHTALL   561
SLIM   414
SLIME   258
SLIP   252, 540
SLIPPER   149
SLITGUT   217
SLOTH   18, 30, 47, 205, 230, 237, 302, 311
SLOVENLINESS   547
SLUBBER   188
SLUG   381
SLUGGE   414
SLUR   762
SLUTTISHNESS   290
SLY   120, 203
SMALL ABILITY   56
SMALLBRAYNE   11
SMALLFAITH   711
SMALL-SHANKS   292
SMELLING   4, 202, 208, 239, 311, 335, 496, 514
SMELT   263
SMIRDIS   56
SMIRKE   364
SMITH   119, 161, 614
SMITH(S)   37, 115, 118, 137, 153, 162, 189, 264, 303, 313, 361, 421, 457, 476, 583, 617, 638, 661, 736, 740, 769, 772, 807
SMITHFIELD   455
SMOKE   153
SMOOTHALL   831
SMOTHERER(S)   119, 142
SMUG   264, 320
SMYRNA/SMYRNAN(S)   605, 745
SNAIL   297
SNAIL(S)   37
SNAP   58, 574, 643, 704
SNARE   167
SNARL   461
SNEAK   167, 630, 631
SNEAKUP   721
SNIP   481, 801
SNOORD   149
SNORE   507
SNOUT   170
SNOW   452
SNUFF   56, 293
SNUG   170
SOAKER   693

WILDFIRE   773
WILDING   523
WILFUL   21.5
WILFUL WAYWARDNESS   11
WILFULNESS   11
WILKIN   194, 512
WILL (*PROPER NAME*)   58, 85, 107, 119, 120, 126, 155, 161, 167, 173, 180, 182, 189, 212, 225, 228, 234, 242, 248, 292, 299, 323, 523, 540, 586, 587, 597, 693, 719, 739, 773, 808, 829
WILL   3, 11, 27, 55, 63, 93, 497
WILL-DOE   474
WILLFUL WANTON   70
WILLIAM   72, 96, 101, 102, 113, 114, 119, 121, 126, 129, 136, 138, 140, 142, 154, 158, 166, 180, 187, 195, 202, 203, 212, 215, 217, 220, 224, 242, 249, 262, 285, 292, 316, 335, 337, 383, 394, 399, 400, 465, 491, 518, 520, 542, 632, 644, 686, 692, 693, 739, 829
WILLIAM THE CONQUEROR   113
WILLIAMS   165, 182, 215
WILLING-TO-WIN-WORSHIP   70
WILLOUGHBY   141
WILLOWBY   451
WILTON   510
WILTSHIRE   129, 142, 512, 824
WILY   85, 158
WIN   494, 574
WINCHESTER   119, 129, 180, 182, 189, 215, 256, 302, 399, 400, 451, 740, 749, 801, 822
WINCOTT   484
WIND MILLER(S)   15
WIND NYMPH(S)   734
WINDMILL   488
WINDS   294, 302, 324, 357, 366, 452, 778, 803
WINDSOR   113, 187, 399
WINE   426
WINE-COOPER(S)   320
WINE-POT CRIER(S)   431
WINFIELD   549
WINGFIELD   399
WINGHAM   119
WINIFRID   177, 217, 228, 244, 267, 388, 477, 531, 785, 825
WINLOSE   806
WINLOSS   806
WINNY   494

WINTER   150, 173, 313, 320, 366, 376, 419, 503, 529, 566, 767
WINTERPLUM   720
WINTERSDALE   520
WIN-THE-FIGHT   455
WINTON   302
WINWIFE   455
WISDOM   11, 96, 200, 202, 208, 367, 383, 495, 496, 500, 571
WISE WOMAN(WOMEN)   535
WISEACRES   465, 520
WISPE   617
WIT   11, 27, 55, 57, 93, 5
WITCH(ES)   119, 123, 125, 156, 182, 231, 280, 287, 327, 399, 404, 449, 450, 485, 494, 497, 501, 527, 535, 545, 551, 552, 618, 654, 785
WITCHCORDIA   545
WITGOOD   262
WITNESS(ES)   109, 189, 560, 568, 638, 743, 762, 810
WITS   4
WITTENBERG   205, 364
WITTIPOL   457
WITTY LOVER(S)   437
WITTYPATE   666
WITWUD   711
WIZARD(S)   424, 646
WOLF   217
WOLF(VES)   420, 488
WOLFGANG   571
WOLSEY   189, 212, 400
WONDER   181, 607
WONDEROSA   434
WOOD (*PROPER NAME*)   242
WOOD   625
WOOD GOD(S)   768
WOOD NYMPH(S)   339, 362, 454, 731, 732
WOODCOCK   188, 474
WOODEVILLE   138, 142, 399
WOODFORD   824
WOODHAMORE   462
WOODMAN(MEN) (*SEE* FORESTER(S))   83, 164, 235, 317, 318, 363, 533, 618, 742
WOODROFF   158, 817
WOOER(S) (*SEE* SUITOR(S))   301, 492
WOOLASTONE   679, 687, 688
WOOLEN DRAPER(S)   224, 721
WOOLFORT   643

Section III
Finding List

The following list comprises all plays indexed. For each play we include the following information:

1) its identifying number, as in W. W. Greg, *A Bibliography of English Printed Drama to the Restoration*, 4 vols. (London: The Bibliographical Society, 1939–58);
2) its title, as in Greg;
3) its author or authors, as in Alfred Harbage, *Annals of English Drama, 975–1700*, revised by Samuel Schoenbaum (Philadelphia: University of Pennsylvania Press, 1964), or as emended by Schoenbaum in his supplements (*Supplement to the Revised Edition* [Evanston, Ill.: Department of English of Northwestern University, 1966], and *A Second Supplement to the Revised Edition* [Evanston, Ill.: Department of English of Northwestern University, 1970]);
4) its date of first publication, as in Greg;
5) its date of first production, as in Harbage and Schoenbaum (H-S);
6) the STC number of the earliest edition of the play, as in either A.W. Pollard and G.R. Redgrave, *A Short-Title Catalogue of Books Printed in England, Scotland, and Ireland, and of English Books Printed Abroad, 1475–1640* (London: The Bibliographical Society, 1926), or as in Donald Wing, *A Short-Title Catalogue of Books Printed in England, Scotland, Ireland, Wales, and British America and of English Books Printed in Other Countries, 1641–1700*, 3 vols. (New York: The Index Society, 1945–51); when the first edition of the play is in doubt, the STC number corresponds to Greg's first entry.

GREG #	PLAY	AUTHOR	GREG DATE	H-S DATE	STC
1	1 Fulgens and Lucrece	Medwall, Henry	about 1512–1516	1497	17778
2	2 Fulgens and Lucrece	Medwall, Henry	about 1512–1516	1497	17778
3	Hycke Scorner	Anon.	?1515–6	1513	14039
4	The Summoning of Every Man (Every Man)	Anon.	1510–?1519	1519	10604
5	The World and the Child	Anon.	17 July 1522	1508	25982
6	The Nature of the Four Elements	Rastell, John	about 1526–7	1517	20722
7	Temperance	Anon.	? about 1528	1535	none
8	1 Gentleness and Nobility	Rastell, J. (?) (Heywood, J., also suggested)	?1529	1527	20723
9	2 Gentleness and Nobility	Rastell, J. (?) (Heywood, J., also suggested)	?1529	1527	20723
10	The Beauty and Good Properties of Women as also their Vices and Evil Conditions [Calisto and Melebea]	Rastell, John (?)	?1530	1527	20721
11	Magnificence	Skelton, John	?1530	1515	22607
12	Andria	Anon.	about 1530	1520	23894
13	Johan Johan, Tib, and Sir Johan	Heywood, John (?)	12 Feb. 1533?	1520	13298

GREG #	PLAY	AUTHOR	GREG DATE	H-S DATE	STC
14	The Pardoner and the Friar	Heywood, John (?)	5 Apr. 1533	1519	13299
14.5	[Old Christmas, or Good Order]	Anon. (Skelton, J.?)	1533	1533	none
15	The Play of the Weather	Heywood, John	1533	1528	13305
16	The Play of Love	Heywood, John	1534	1533	13303
17	1 Nature	Medwall, Henry	?1530–1534	1495	17779
18	2 Nature	Medwall, Henry	?1530–1534	1495	17779
19	[Pater Filius et Vxor, or The Prodigal Son]	Anon.	?1530–1534	1530	none
20	Youth	Anon.	1530?–1535	1520	14111
21	The Four P's	Heywood, John	? about 1544	1520	13300
21.5	The Four Cardinal Virtues	Anon.	1541–7	1542	none
22	The Chief Promises of God	Bale, John	about 1547–8	1538	1305
23	The Temptation of Christ	Bale, John	about 1547–8	1538	1279
24	The Three Laws	Bale, John	about 1547–8	1538	1287
25	[Somebody and Others, or The Spoiling of Lady Verity]	Anon.	about 1547–1550	1550	none
26	Johan the Evangelist	Anon.	? about 1550	1520	14643
27	Wealth and Health	Anon.	? about 1565	1554	14110
28	Troas	Heywood, Jasper	about 14 Jan. 1559	1559	22227

GREG #	PLAY	AUTHOR	GREG DATE	H-S DATE	STC
29	Thyestes	Heywood, Jasper	26 Mar. 1560	1560	22226
30	Impatient Poverty	Anon.	10 June 1560	1547	14114
31	Nice Wanton	Anon.	10 June 1560	1550	25016
32	Robin Hood	Anon.	?30 Nov. 1560	1560	13691
33	Godly Queen Hester	Anon.	about Feb. 1561	1527	13251
34	Hercules Furens	Heywood, Jasper	1561	1561	22223
35	Jack Juggler	Anon.	about Nov. 1562	1555	14837
36	Oedipus	Neville, Alexander	28 Apr. 1563	1563	22225
37	Thersites	Udall, Nicholas (?)	1561–1563	1537	23949
38	Albion Knight	Anon.	about Aug. 1565	1537	275
39	Ferrex and Porrex (Gorboduc)	Norton, T.; Sackville, T.	22 Sept. 1565	1562	18684
40	Darius	Anon.	Oct. 1565	1565	6277
41	Lusty Juventus	Wever, R.	about 1565	1550	25149
42	Agamemnon	Studley, John	about Feb. 1566	1566	22222

GREG #	PLAY	AUTHOR	GREG DATE	H-S DATE	STC
43	The Cruel Debtor	Wager, [W.?]	about Mar. 1566	1565	24934
44	Medea	Studley, John	about June 1566	1566	22224
45	Octavia	Nuce, Thomas	22 July–20 Aug. 1566	1566	22229
46	Ralph Roister Doister	Udall, Nicholas	about Oct. 1566?	1552	24508
47	The Repentance of Mary Magdalene	Wager, Lewis	about Dec. 1566	1558	24932
48	The Interlude of Vice [Horestes]	Pickering, John	1567	1567	19917
49	The Trial of Treasure	Wager, W. (?)	1567	1567	24271
50	Like Will to Like	Fulwell, Ulpian	about Sept. 1568	1568	11473
51	Jacob and Esau	Udall, N. (?) or Hunnis, W. (?)	1568	1554	14327
52	Patient Grissil	Phillip, John	? about Feb. 1569	1559	19865
53	The Longer thou Livest the More Fool thou Art	Wager, W.	about Apr. 1569	1559	24935
54	The Disobedient Child	Ingelend, Thomas	? about Aug. 1569	1560	14085

GREG #	PLAY	AUTHOR	GREG DATE	H-S DATE	STC
55	The Marriage of Wit and Science	Anon.	about Aug. 1569	1568	17466
56	Cambyses	Preston, Thomas	about Oct. 1569	1561	20287
57	Enough is as Good as a Feast	Wager, W.	about 1565–1570	1560	24933
58	Damon and Pythias	Edwards, Richard	1571	1565	7514
59	New Custom	Anon.	1573	1571	6150
60	Supposes	Gascoigne, George	(collection) 1573	1566	11635
61	Jocasta	Gascoigne, G.; Kinwelmershe, F.	(collection) 1573	1566	11635
62	The Masque for Lord Montacute	Gascoigne, George	(collection) 1573	1572	11635
63	Free-Will	Cheke, Henry	?1573	1568	18419
64	The Interlude of Minds	Anon.	? about 1574	1574	18550
65	Appius and Virginia	B[ower?], R[ichard?]	1575	1564	1059
66	The Entertainment at Bristow	Churchyard, T.; Roberts, J.	1575	1574	5232

GREG #	PLAY	AUTHOR	GREG DATE	H-S DATE	STC
67	Gammer Gurton's Needle	Stevenson, W. (?) (revised by Bridges, J.?)	1575	1553	23263
68	The Glass of Government	Gascoigne, George	1575	1575	11643
69	Common Conditions	Anon.	26 July 1576	1576	5592
70	The Tide Tarrieth no Man	Wapull, George	22 Oct. 1576	1576	25018
71	Abraham's Sacrifice	Golding, Arthur	1577	1575	2047
72	All for Money	Lupton, Thomas	(25 Nov. 1577) 1578	1577	16949
73	1 Promus and Cassandra	Whetstone, George	20 Aug. 1578	1578	25347
74	2 Promus and Cassandra	Whetstone, George	20 Aug. 1578	1578	25347
75	The Entertainment at Norwich	Churchyard; Garter, B.; Golding-ham, H.	30 Aug. 1578	1578	11627
76	The Entertainment in Suffolk and Norfolk	Churchyard; Garter, B; Golding-ham, H.	20 Sept. 1578	1578	5226
76.5	The Most Virtuous and Godly Susanna	Garter, Thomas	1578	1569	11632a

GREG #	PLAY	AUTHOR	GREG DATE	H-S DATE	STC
77	The Entertainment of the French Ambassadors [The Fortress of Perfect Beauty]	Goldwell, Henry (describer)	1 July 1581	1581	11990
78	The Conflict of Conscience	Woodes, Nathaniel	1581	1572	25966
79	Thebais	Newton, Thomas	(collection) 1581	1581	22221
80	Hippolytus	Studley, John	(collection) 1581	1567	22221
81	Hercules Oetaeus	Studley, John	(collection) 1581	1566	22221
82	Sappho and Phao	Lyly, John	6 Apr. 1584	1584	17086
83	The Arraignment of Paris	Peele, George	1584	1581	19530
84	Campaspe (Alexander, Campaspe, and Diogenes)	Lyly, John	1584	1584	17048b
85	The Three Ladies of London	Wilson, Robert	1584	1581	25784
86	Fedele and Fortunio	Anon. (Munday, A.?)	(12 Nov. 1584) 1585	1584	19447
87	The Pageant for Wolstan Dixie	Peele, George	29 Oct. 1585	1585	19533
88	The Entertainment at Woodstock	Gascoigne, G. (?) or Lee, H.(?)	1585	1575	7596

GREG #	PLAY	AUTHOR	GREG DATE	H-S DATE	STC
89	The Misfortunes of Arthur	Hughes, T.; with Bacon; Trotte; Fulbeck; Lancaster; Yelverton; Penroodock; Flower	(28 Feb.– 24 Mar. 1588) 1587	1588	13921
90	The Entertainment at Kenilworth	Gascoigne; with Hunnis; Ferrers; Goldingham, H.; Badger; Paten (?); Mulcaster (?)	(collection) 1587	1575	11638
91	Andria	Kyffin, Maurice	1588	1588	23895
92	Love and Fortune	Anon. (Munday, A.?)	1589	1582	24286
93	The Three Lords of London	Wilson, Robert	31 July 1590	1588	25783
94	1 Tamburlaine	Marlowe, Christopher	14 Aug. 1590	1587	17425
95	2 Tamburlaine	Marlowe, Christopher	14 Aug. 1590	1588	17425
96	The Pageant for John Allot	Nelson, Thomas	29 Oct. 1590	1590	18423

GREG #	PLAY	AUTHOR	GREG DATE	H-S DATE	STC
97	Amyntas' Pastoral	Fraunce, Abraham	9 Feb. 1591	1591	11340
98	The Entertainment at Elvetham	Breton, N. (& Lyly, J.?)	1 Oct. 1591	1591	7583
99	Endymion	Lyly, John	4 Oct. 1591	1588	17050
100	Descensus Astraeae	Peele, George	29 Oct. 1591	1591	19532
101	1 [The Troublesome Reign of] King John	Anon. (Peele, G.?)	1591	1588	14644
102	2 [The Troublesome Reign of] King John	Anon. (Peele, G.?)	1591	1588	14645
103	The Entertainment at Cowdray	Anon. (Lyly, J.?)	(after 20 Aug.) 1591	1591	3903
104	Tancred and Gismund	Wilmot, R.; Stafford; Hatton; Noel; Al., G.	about Dec. 1591	1566	25764
105	Gallathea	Lyly, John	(4 Oct. 1591) 1592	1585	17080
106	Midas	Lyly, John	(4 Oct. 1591) 1592	1589	17083
107	Arden of Feversham	Anon. (Kyd, T.?)	3 Apr. 1592	1591	733
108	Antonius (Antony)	Herbert, Mary	3 May 1592	1590	18138

GREG #	PLAY	AUTHOR	GREG DATE	H-S DATE	STC
109	Soliman and Perseda	Anon. (Kyd, T.?)	20 Nov. 1592	1592	22894
110	The Spanish Tragedy	Kyd, T. (lost additions by Jonson, B.)	(before 18 Dec.) 1592	1587	15086
111	The Entertainments at Bisham, Sudeley, and Rycote	Anon. (Lyly, J.?)	(after 2 Oct.) 1592	1592	7600
112	Edward the First	Peele, George	about 8 Oct. 1593	1591	19535
113	Fair Em	Anon. (Wilson, R.?)	?1593	1590	7675
114	Jack Straw	Anon.	(23 Oct. 1593) 1594	1591	23356
115	A Knack to Know a Knave	Anon. (Kempe? Peele? Wilson?)	7 Jan. 1594	1592	15027
116	Cornelia (Pompey the Great his fair Cornelia's Tragedy)	Kyd, Thomas	26 Jan. 1594	1594	11622
117	Titus Andronicus	Shakespeare, William (reviser?)	6 Feb. 1594	1594	22328
118	A Looking-Glass for London and England	Greene, R.; Lodge, T.	5 Mar. 1594	1590	16679
119	2 Henry the Sixth (The First Part of the Contention of York and Lancaster)	Shakespeare, William	12 Mar. 1594	1591	26099

GREG #	PLAY	AUTHOR	GREG DATE	H-S DATE	STC
120	The Taming of the Shrew (The Taming of a Shrew)	Anon. (poss. Shake-speare, W.)	2 May 1594	1589	23667
121	Friar Bacon and Friar Bongay	Greene, Robert	14 May 1594	1589	12267
122	The Wounds of Civil War	Lodge, Thomas	24 May 1594	1588	16678
123	Orlando Furioso	Greene, R. (& Rowley, S.?)	28 May 1594	1591	12265
124	The Cobbler's Prophecy	Wilson, Robert	8 June 1594	1590	25781
125	Mother Bombie	Lyly, John	18 June 1594	1589	17084
126	[The True Tragedy of] Richard the Third	Anon.	19 June 1594	1591	21009
127	The Battle of Alcazar	Peele, George	1594	1589	19531
128	Dido	Marlowe, C.; Nashe, T.	(before 22 Apr.) 1594	1587	17441
129	Edward the Second	Marlowe, Christopher	1594	1592	17437
130	1 Selimus	Greene, Robert (?)	1594	1592	12310a
131	The Wars of Cyrus	Anon.	1594	1588	6160
132	Cleopatra	Daniel, Samuel	(collection) 1594	1593	6254
133	The Massacre at Paris	Marlowe, Chris-topher	?1594	1593	17423

GREG #	PLAY	AUTHOR	GREG DATE	H-S DATE	STC
134	The Pedlar's Prophecy	Anon.	(about 13 May 1594) 1595	1561	25782
135	Menaechmi	Warner, William	(10 June 1594) 1595	1592	20002
136	Locrine	'W.S.' (Peele? Greene?)	(20 July 1594) 1595	1591	21528
137	The Old Wives Tale	Peele, George	16 Apr. 1595	1590	19545
138	3 Henry the Sixth ([The True Tragedy of] Richard Duke of York)	Shakespeare, William	1595	1591	21006
139	A Knack to Know an Honest Man	Anon. (Munday? Heywood?)	(26 Nov. 1595) 1596	1594	15028
140	Edward the Third	Anon. (Shakespeare in part?)	(1 Dec. 1595) 1596	1590	7501
141	Richard the Second	Shakespeare, William	29 Aug. 1597	1595	22307
142	Richard the Third	Shakespeare, William	20 Oct. 1597	1593	22314
143	Romeo and Juliet	Shakespeare, William	1597	1595	22322
144	The Woman in the Moon	Lyly, John	1597	1593	17090
145	1 Henry the Fourth	Shakespeare, William	25 Feb. 1598	1597	22280

GREG #	PLAY	AUTHOR	GREG DATE	H-S DATE	STC
146	The Blind Beggar of Alexandria	Chapman, George	about 15 Aug. 1598	1596	4965
147	The Virtuous Octavia	Brandon, Samuel	5 Oct. 1598	1598	3544
148	The Famous Victories of Henry the Fifth	Anon. (Tarlton? Rowley, S.?)	1598	1586	13072
149	James the Fourth [The Scottish History]	Greene, Robert	1598	1590	12308
150	Love's Labour's Lost	Shakespeare, William	1598	1595	22294
151	Mucedorus and Amadine	Anon.	1598	1590	18230
152	The Entertainment at Wanstead [The Lady of May]	Sidney, Philip	(collection) 1598	1578	22541
153	1 Edward the Fourth	Heywood, T. (?), and others(?)	28 Aug. 1599	1599	13341
154	2 Edward the Fourth	Heywood, T. (?), and others(?)	28 Aug. 1599	1599	13341
155	A Warning for Fair Women	Anon. (Heywood, T.?)	17 Nov. 1599	1599	25089
156	Alphonsus of Aragon	Greene, Robert	1599	1587	12233
157	Clyomon and Clamydes	Anon. (Preston, T.?)	1599	1570	5450a

GREG #	PLAY	AUTHOR	GREG DATE	H-S DATE	STC
158	George a Green	Greene, Robert (?)	1599	1590	12212
159	An Humorous Day's Mirth	Chapman, George	1599	1597	4987
160	The Love of David and Fair Bethsabe	Peele, George	1599	1587	19540
161	The Two Angry Women of Abingdon	Porter, Henry	1599	1588	20123
162	Old Fortunatus	Dekker, Thomas	20 Feb. 1600	1599	6517
163	Every Man out of his Humour	Jonson, Ben	8 Apr. 1600	1599	14767
164	The Maid's Metamorphosis	Anon. (Day? Lyly?)	24 July 1600	1600	17188
165	Henry the Fifth	Shakespeare, William	about 4 Aug. 1600	1599	22289
166	1 Sir John Oldcastle	Drayton; Hathway; Munday; Wilson	11 Aug. 1600	1599	18795
167	2 Henry the Fourth	Shakespeare, William	23 Aug. 1600	1597	22288
168	Much Ado about Nothing	Shakespeare, William	23 Aug. 1600	1598	22304
169	The Wisdom of Doctor Dodypoll	Anon.	7 Oct. 1600	1599	6991
170	A Midsummer-Night's Dream	Shakespeare, William	8 Oct. 1600	1595	22302
171	The Weakest Goeth to the Wall	Anon. (Dekker, T., in part?)	23 Oct. 1600	1600	25144

GREG #	PLAY	AUTHOR	GREG DATE	H-S DATE	STC
172	The Merchant of Venice	Shakespeare, William	28 Oct. 1600	1596	22296
173	Summer's Last Will and Testament	Nashe, Thomas	28 Oct. 1600	1592	18376
174	Look About You	Anon. (poss. Chettle, Dekker, or Wadeson)	1600	1599	16799
175	The Shoemakers' Holiday	Dekker, Thomas	1600	1599	6523
176	Every Man in his Humour	Jonson, Ben	(14 Aug. 1600) 1601	1598	14766
177	Jack Drum's Entertainment	Marston, John	(23 Oct. 1600) 1601	1600	7243
178	Love's Metamorphosis	Lyly, John	(25 Nov. 1600) 1601	1590	17082
179	The Downfall of Robert Earl of Huntingdon	Chettle, H.; Munday, A.	(1 Dec. 1600) 1601	1598	18271
180	The Death of Robert Earl of Huntingdon	Chettle, H.; Munday, A.	(1 Dec. 1600) 1601	1598	18269
181	Cynthia's Revels (The Fountain of Self-Love)	Jonson, Ben	23 May 1601	1601	14773
182	Two Lamentable Tragedies	Yarington, Robert	1601	1594	26076
183	Il Pastor Fido	Dymock, John (?)	(16 Sept. 1601) 1602	1601	12415

GREG #	PLAY	AUTHOR	GREG DATE	H-S DATE	STC
184	Antonio and Mellida	Marston, John	(24 Oct. 1601) 1602	1599	17473
185	Antonio's Revenge	Marston, John	(24 Oct. 1601) 1602	1600	17474
186	Poetaster	Jonson, Ben	(21 Dec. 1601) 1602	1601	14781
187	The Merry Wives of Windsor (Sir John Falstaff)	Shakespeare, William	18 Jan. 1602	1600	22299
188	Blurt Master-Constable	Anon. (Middleton? Dekker?)	7 June 1602	1601	17876
189	Thomas Lord Cromwell	Anon. (by 'W.S.')	11 Aug. 1602	1600	21532
190	The Contention between Liberality and Prodigality	Anon.	1602	1601	5593
191	How a Man may Choose a Good Wife from a Bad	Heywood, T. (?) ('Joshua Cooke' now rejected)	1602	1602	5594
192	A Larum for London	Anon.	1602	1599	16754
193	The Satire of the Three Estates	Lindsay, David	1602	1540	15681
194	The Satire of the Three Estates	Lindsay, David	1602	1540	15681
195	Satiromastix	Dekker, T. (with Marston, J.?)	1602	1601	6521

GREG #	PLAY	AUTHOR	GREG DATE	H-S DATE	STC
196	Darius	Alexander, William	(after 24 Mar.) 1603	1603	349
197	Hamlet	Shakespeare, William	(after 19 May) 1603	1601	22275
198	Patient Grissil	Chettle; Dekker; Haughton	1603	1600	6518
199	Philotus	Anon. (Montgomery? Sempill?)	1603	1603	19888
200	The Entertainment through London [Jonson's Part]	Jonson, Ben	19 Mar. 1604	1604	14756
201	The Entertainment at Althorp [The Satyr]	Jonson, Ben	19 Mar. 1604	1603	14756
202	The Entertainment through London [Dekker's Magnificent Entertainment]	Dekker, T. (Zeal's speech by Middleton)	2 Apr. 1604	1604	6510
203	The Malcontent	Marston, J. (additions by Webster)	5 July 1604	1604	17479
204	1 The Honest Whore (The Converted Courtesan)	Dekker, T., with Middleton, T.	9 Nov. 1604	1604	6501
205	Doctor Faustus	Marlowe, C. (& Rowley, S.?)	1604	1592	17429
206	The Wit of a Woman	Anon.	1604	1604	25868

GREG #	PLAY	AUTHOR	GREG DATE	H-S DATE	STC
207	The Vision of the Twelve Goddesses (The Masque at Hampton Court)	Daniel, Samuel	(after 8 Jan.) 1604	1604	6264
208	The Entertainment through London [Harrison's Arches of Triumph]	Dekker; Harrison; Webster	(after 16 June) 1604	1604	12863
209	Croesus	Alexander, William	(collection) 1604	1604	343
210	The Trial of Chivalry (This Gallant Cavaliero Dick Bowyer)	Anon. (Heywood? Chettle?)	(4 Dec. 1604) 1605	1601	24935a
211	The Fair Maid of Bristow	Anon.	8 Feb. 1605	1604	3794
212	When you See me you Know me	Rowley, Samuel	12 Feb. 1605	1604	21417
213	King Leir	Anon.	8 May 1605	1590	15343
214	The Dutch Courtesan	Marston, John	26 June 1605	1604	17475
215	1 If you Know not Me you Know Nobody	Heywood, Thomas	5 July 1605	1604	13328
216	Sejanus his Fall	Jonson, Ben	6 Aug. 1605	1603	14782
217	Eastward Ho	Chapman; Jonson; Marston	4 Sept. 1605	1605	4970
218	The Triumphs of Reunited Britannia	Munday, Anthony	29 Oct. 1605	1605	18279
219	All Fools	Chapman, George	1605	1604	4963

GREG #	PLAY	AUTHOR	GREG DATE	H-S DATE	STC
220	Captain Thomas Stukeley	Anon. (Heywood, T., in part?)	1605	1596	23405
221	1 Jeronimo	Anon. (Kyd, T.?)	1605	1604	15085
222	The London Prodigal	Anon. ('William Shake-speare'; Dekker? Drayton? or Marston?)	1605	1604	22333
223	Philotas	Daniel, Samuel	(collection) 1605	1604	6239
224	2 If you Know not Me you Know Nobody (2 Queen Elizabeth's Troubles)	Heywood, Thomas	(14 Sept. 1605) 1606	1605	13336
225	The Return from Parnassus [The Scourge of Simony]	Anon. (Gwyn, O., in part?)	(16 Oct. 1605) 1606	1603	19309
226	The Gentleman Usher	Chapman, George	(26 Nov. 1605) 1606	1602	4978
227	The Queen's Arcadia	Daniel, Samuel	(26 Nov. 1605) 1606	1605	6262
228	Sir Giles Goosecap	Chapman, George	10 Jan. 1606	1602	12050
229	Nobody and Somebody	Anon.	12 Mar. 1606	1605	18597
230	Parasitaster	Marston, John	12 Mar. 1606	1605	17483

GREG #	PLAY	AUTHOR	GREG DATE	H-S DATE	STC
231	The Wonder of Women (Sophonisba)	Marston, John	17 Mar. 1606	1605	17488
232	Caesar and Pompey [Caesar's Revenge]	Anon.	5 June 1606	1595	4339
233	The Entertainment of the King of Denmark	Anon.	8 Aug. 1606	1606	5194
234	Wily Beguiled	Anon. (poss. Rowley, S.)	12 Nov. 1606	1602	25818
235	The Isle of Gulls	Day, John	1606	1606	6412
236	Monsieur D'Olive	Chapman, George	1606	1604	4983
237	Hymenaei	Jonson, Ben	(after 6 Jan.) 1606	1606	14774
238	The Masque at Lord Hay's Marriage	Campion, Thomas	26 Jan. 1607	1607	4538
239	Lingua	Tomkis, Thomas	23 Feb. 1607	1607	24104
240	Claudius Tiberius Nero [Tiberius]	Anon.	10 Apr. 1607	1607	24063
241	The Whore of Babylon	Dekker, Thomas	20 Apr. 1607	1606	6532
242	The Fair Maid of the Exchange	Anon. (Heywood, T.?)	24 Apr. 1607	1602	13317
243	The Phoenix	Middleton, Thomas	9 May 1607	1604	17892
244	Michaelmas Term	Middleton, Thomas	15 May 1607	1606	17890

GREG #	PLAY	AUTHOR	GREG DATE	H-S DATE	STC
245	The Woman Hater	Beaumont, F., with Fletcher, J.	20 May 1607	1606	1692
246	Bussy D'Ambois	Chapman, George	3 June 1607	1604	4966
247	Cupid's Whirligig	Sharpham, Edward	29 June 1607	1607	22380
248	The Travels of the Three English Brothers	Day; Rowley, W.; Wilkins	29 June 1607	1607	6417
249	The Miseries of Enforced Marriage	Wilkins, George	31 July 1607	1606	25635
250	Northward Ho	Dekker, T.; Webster, J.	6 Aug. 1607	1605	6539
251	The Puritan	Anon. (by 'W.S.'; Middleton, T.?)	6 Aug. 1607	1606	21531
252	What you Will	Marston, John	6 Aug. 1607	1601	17487
253	The Revenger's Tragedy	Anon. (Tourneur? Middleton?)	7 Oct. 1607	1606	24149
254	The Devil's Charter	Barnes, Barnabe	16 Oct. 1607	1607	1466
255	The Fleer	Sharpham, Edward	1607	1606	22384

GREG #	PLAY	AUTHOR	GREG DATE	H-S DATE	STC
256	Sir Thomas Wyatt	Dekker; Webster (& others?)	1607	1604	6537
257	Westward Ho	Dekker, T., with Webster, J.	1607	1604	6540
258	A Woman Killed with Kindness	Heywood, Thomas	1607	1603	13371
259	Volpone	Jonson, Ben	(after 11 Feb.) 1607	1606	14783
260	The Alexandrean Tragedy	Alexander, William	(collection) 1607	1607	344
261	Julius Caesar	Alexander, William	(collection) 1607	1607	344
262	A Trick to Catch the Old One	Middleton, Thomas	(7 Oct. 1607) 1608	1605	17896
263	The Family of Love	Middleton, T. (& Dekker, T.?)	(12 Oct. 1607) 1608	1602	17879
264	The Merry Devil of Edmonton	Anon. (poss. Dekker, T.)	(22 Oct. 1607) 1608	1602	7493
265	King Lear	Shakespeare, William	(26 Nov. 1607) 1608	1605	22292
266	Your Five Gallants	Middleton, Thomas	22 Mar. 1608	1605	17907

GREG #	PLAY	AUTHOR	GREG DATE	H-S DATE	STC
267	Law Tricks	Day, J. (with Wilkins, G.?)	28 Mar. 1608	1604	6416
268	Humour out of Breath	Day, John	12 Apr. 1608	1608	6411
269	The Masque of Blackness	Jonson, Ben	21 Apr. 1608	1605	14761
270	The Masque of Beauty	Jonson, Ben	21 Apr. 1608	1608	14761
271	The Masque at Lord Haddington's Marriage [The Hue and Cry after Cupid]	Jonson, Ben	21 Apr. 1608	1608	14761
272	A Yorkshire Tragedy	Anon. ('W. Shakespeare'; Wilkins?)	2 May 1608	1606	22340
273	The Rape of Lucrece	Heywood, Thomas	3 June 1608	1607	13360
274	The Conspiracy of Charles Duke of Byron	Chapman, George	5 June 1608	1608	4968
275	The Tragedy of Charles Duke of Byron	Chapman, George	5 June 1608	1608	4968
276	A Mad World my Masters	Middleton, Thomas	4 Oct. 1608	1606	17888
277	The Dumb Knight	Markham, G.; Machin, L.	6 Oct. 1608	1608	17398
278	Mustapha	Greville, Fulke	(25 Nov. 1608) 1609	1596	12362

GREG #	PLAY	AUTHOR	GREG DATE	H-S DATE	STC
279	Troilus and Cressida (Troilus and Cresseid)	Shakespeare, William	28 Jan. 1609	1602	22331
280	The Masque of Queens	Jonson, Ben	22 Feb. 1609	1609	14778
281	The Case is Altered	Jonson, Ben	20 July 1609	1597	14757
282	Camp-Bell	Munday, Anthony	30 Oct. 1609	1609	18265
283	Every Woman in her Humour	Machin, Lewis (?)	1609	1607	25948
284	Pericles	Shakespeare, W. (reviser? collaborator? Wilkins, G., now rejected)	1609	1608	22334
285	The Two Maids of Moreclacke	Armin, Robert	1609	1608	773
286	The Turk (Muleasses the Turk)	Mason, John	(10 Mar. 1609) 1610	1607	17617
287	The Faithful Shepherdess	Fletcher, John	before June 1610	1608	11068
288	Chester's Triumph	Amerie, R.; Davies, R.	12 June 1610	1610	5118
289	London's Love to Prince Henry	Munday, Anthony	31 May–29 Oct. 1610	1610	13159

GREG #	PLAY	AUTHOR	GREG DATE	H-S DATE	STC
290	Histriomastix	Marston, J. (reviser?) and others(?)	31 Oct. 1610	1599	13529
291	Tethys' Festival	Daniel, Samuel	(after 5 June) 1610	1610	13161
292	Ram Alley	Barry, Lording	(9 Nov. 1610) 1611	1608	1502
293	The Atheist's Tragedy	Tourneur, Cyril	14 Sept. 1611	1611	24146
294	The Golden Age	Heywood, Thomas	14 Oct. 1611	1610	13325
295	Chrusothriambos	Munday, Anthony	29 Oct. 1611	1611	18267
296	Catiline his Conspiracy	Jonson, Ben	1611	1611	14759
297	May Day	Chapman, George	1611	1602	4980
298	The Roaring Girl	Dekker, T.; Middleton, T.	1611	1608	17908
299	A Woman is a Weathercock	Field, Nathan	(23 Nov. 1611) 1612	1609	10854
300	A Christian Turned Turk	Daborne, Robert	1 Feb. 1612	1610	6184

GREG #	PLAY	AUTHOR	GREG DATE	H-S DATE	STC
301	The Widow's Tears	Chapman, George	17 Apr. 1612	1605	4994
302	Troia Noua Triumphans	Dekker, Thomas	29 Oct. 1612	1612	6530
303	The Alchemist	Jonson, Ben	1612	1610	14755
304	Epicene (The Silent Woman)	Jonson, Ben	1612	1609	14751
305	If it be not Good the Devil is in it	Dekker, T. (with Daborne, R.?)	1612	1611	6507
306	The White Devil (Vittoria Corombona)	Webster, John	1612	1612	25178
307	The Revenge of Bussy D'Ambois	Chapman, George	(17 Apr. 1612) 1613	1610	4989
308	Mariam	Cary, Elizabeth	'(17 Dec. 1612) 1613	1604	4613
309	The Masque of the Inner Temple and Gray's Inn	Beaumont, Francis	27 Feb. 1613	1613	1663
310	The Masque of the Middle Temple and Lincoln's Inn	Chapman, George	27 Feb. 1613	1613	4981
311	The Triumphs of Truth	Middleton, Thomas	3 Nov. 1613	1613	17903
312	The Entertainment on Michaelmas Day 1613	Middleton, Thomas	3 Nov. 1613	1613	17904
313	The Brazen Age	Heywood, Thomas	1613	1611	13310

GREG #	PLAY	AUTHOR	GREG DATE	H-S DATE	STC
314	Cynthia's Revenge	Stephens, John	1613	1613	23248
315	The Insatiate Countess	Marston, J.; Barkstead, W.	1613	1610	17476
316	The Knight of the Burning Pestle	Beaumont, F. (with Fletcher, J.?)	1613	1607	1674
317	The Silver Age	Heywood, Thomas	1613	1611	13365
318	The Entertainment at Cawsome	Campion, Thomas	(after 28 Apr.) 1613	1613	4545
319	The Lords' Masque	Campion, Thomas	(after 28 Apr.) 1613	1613	4545
320	The Masque of Flowers	Anon. (dedication signed 'I. G., W.D., T.B.')	21 Jan. 1614	1614	17625
321	The Hog hath Lost his Pearl	Tailor, Robert	23 May 1614	1613	23658
322	Himatia Poleos	Munday, Anthony	29 Oct. 1614	1614	18274
323	Greene's Tu Quoque	Cooke, John	1614	1611	5673
324	The Masque at the Earl of Somerset's Marriage [The Masque of Squires]	Campion, Thomas	1614	1613	4539

GREG #	PLAY	AUTHOR	GREG DATE	H-S DATE	STC
325	Hymen's Triumph	Daniel, Samuel	13 Jan. 1615	1614	6257
326	Exchange Ware at the Second Hand (Band, Cuff, and Ruffe)	Anon.	10 Feb. 1615	1615	1355
327	The Valiant Welshman	'R.A.' (Armin, R.? Anton, R.?)	21 Feb. 1615	1612	16
328	Cupid's Revenge	Fletcher, J., with Beaumont, F.	24 Apr. 1615	1612	1667
329	The Hector of Germany	Smith, W [entworth?]	24 Apr. 1615	1614	22871
330	Albumazar	Tomkis, Thomas	28 Apr. 1615	1615	24100
331	Work for Cutlers	Anon.	4 July 1615	1615	25981
332	Metropolis Coronata	Munday, Anthony	30 Oct. 1615	1615	18275
333	The Four Prentices of London	Heywood, Thomas	1615	1600	13321
334	The Scornful Lady	Fletcher, J., with Beaumont, F.	19 Mar. 1616	1613	1686
335	Chrysanaleia	Munday, Anthony	29 Oct. 1616	1616	18266
336	Englishmen for my Money (A Woman will have her Will)	Haughton, William	1616	1598	12931
337	The Honest Lawyer	'S.S.'	1616	1615	21519

GREG #	PLAY	AUTHOR	GREG DATE	H-S DATE	STC
338	Ciuitatis Amor	Middleton, Thomas	(after 4 Nov.) 1616	1616	17878
339	The Entertainment at Highgate [The Penates]	Jonson, Ben	(collection) 1616	1604	14751
340	The Entertainment at Theobalds, 1606 [The Hours]	Jonson, Ben	(collection) 1616	1606	14751
341	The Entertainment at Theobalds, 1607 [The Genius]	Jonson, Ben	(collection) 1616	1607	14751
342	Prince Henry's Barriers [The Lady of the Lake]	Jonson, Ben	(collection) 1616	1610	14751
343	Oberon the Faery Prince	Jonson, Ben	(collection) 1616	1611	14751
344	Love Freed from Ignorance and Folly	Jonson, Ben	(collection) 1616	1611	14751
345	Love Restored	Jonson, Ben	(collection) 1616	1612	14751
346	The Challenge at Tilt at a Marriage	Jonson, Ben	(collection) 1616	1613	14751
347	The Irish Masque	Jonson, Ben	(collection) 1616	1613	14751
348	Mercury Vindicated from the Alchemists	Jonson, Ben	(collection) 1616	1616	14751
349	The Golden Age Restored	Jonson, Ben	(collection) 1616	1615	14751

GREG #	PLAY	AUTHOR	GREG DATE	H-S DATE	STC
350	Lovers Made Men (The Masque at Lord Hay's)	Jonson, Ben	22 Feb. 1617	1617	14775
351	The Triumphs of Honour and Industry	Middleton, Thomas	29 Oct. 1617	1617	17899
352	A Fair Quarrel	Middleton, T.; Rowley, W.	1617	1617	17911
353	Τεχνογαμία	Holiday, Barten	20 Apr. 1618	1618	13617
354	See me and See me not	Belchier, Daubridgcourt	3 June 1618	1618	1803
355	Siderothriambos	Munday, Anthony	29 Oct. 1618	1618	18278
356	Amends for Ladies	Field, Nathan	1618	1611	10851
357	The Maid's Tragedy	Beaumont, F., with Fletcher, J.	28 Apr. 1619	1610	1677
358	The Inner Temple Masque [The Masque of Heroes]	Middleton, Thomas	10 July 1619	1619	17887
359	The Triumphs of Love and Antiquity	Middleton, Thomas	29 Oct. 1619	1619	17902
360	A King and no King	Beaumont, F.; Fletcher, J.	1619	1611	1670
361	Two Wise Men and all the Rest Fools	Anon.	1619	1619	4991
362	Swetnam Arraigned by Women	Anon.	(17 Oct. 1619) 1620	1618	23544

GREG #	PLAY	AUTHOR	GREG DATE	H-S DATE	STC
363	Philaster	Beaumont, F., with Fletcher, J.	10 Jan. 1620	1609	1681
364	The Two Merry Milkmaids	'I.C.' (Cumber; John?)	22 May 1620	1619	4281
365	The World Tossed at Tennis	Middletown, T.; Rowley, W.	4 July 1620	1620	17909
366	Τῆς Εἰρήνης Τροπαῖα	Squire, John	30 Oct. 1620	1620	23118
367	The Sun in Aries	Middleton, T. (& Munday, A.?)	29 Oct. 1621	1621	17895
368	Thierry and Theodoret	Fletcher; Massinger (& Beaumont?)	1621	1617	11074
369	The Entertainment at Sir William Cokayne's in Easter Week [The Cock]	Middleton, Thomas	(collection) 1621	1621	17886
370	The Entertainment at Bunhill on the Shooting Day [The Archer]	Middleton, Thomas	(collection) 1621	1621	17886
371	The Entertainment at the Conduit Head [The Water Nymph]	Middleton, Thomas	(collection) 1621	1621	17886
372	The Entertainment for the General Training [Pallas]	Middleton, Thomas	(collection) 1621	1621	17886
373	The Entertainment at Sir William Cokayne's upon Simon and Jude's Day [The Year's Funeral]	Middleton, Thomas	(collection) 1621	1621	17886

GREG #	PLAY	AUTHOR	GREG DATE	H-S DATE	STC
374	The Entertainment at Sir Francis Jones's Welcome [Comus the Great Sir of Feasts]	Middleton, Thomas	(collection) 1621	1621	17886
375	The Entertainment at Sir Francis Jones's at Christmas [The Triumph of Temperance]	Middleton, Thomas	(collection) 1621	1621	17886
376	The Entertainment at Sir Francis Jones's at Easter [The Seasons]	Middleton, Thomas	(collection) 1621	1621	17886
377	The Entertainment of the Lords of the Council by Sheriff Allen [Flora's Welcome]	Middleton, Thomas	(collection) 1621	1621	17886
378	The Entertainment of the Lords of the Council by Sheriff Ducie [Flora's Servants]	Middleton, Thomas	(collection) 1621	1621	17886
379	Othello	Shakespeare, William	(6 Oct. 1621) 1622	1604	22305
380	The Virgin Martyr	Dekker, T.; Massinger, P.	(7 Dec. 1621) 1622	1620	17644
381	The Masque of Augurs	Johnson, Ben	6 Jan. 1622	1622	14777
382	Herod and Antipater	Markham, G.; Sampson, W.	22 Feb. 1622	1622	17401
383	The Triumphs of Honour and Virtue	Middleton, Thomas	29 Oct. 1622	1622	17900
384	The Heir	May, Thomas	1622	1620	17713
385	Time Vindicated	Jonson, Ben	6 Jan. 1623	1623	None

GREG #	PLAY	AUTHOR	GREG DATE	H-S DATE	STC
386	The Duke of Milan	Massinger, Philip	5 May 1623	1621	17634
387	The Triumphs of Integrity	Middleton, Thomas	29 Oct. 1623	1623	17901
388	The Devil's Law Case	Webster, John	1623	1617	25173
389	The Duchess of Malfy	Webster, John	1623	1614	25176
390	The Tempest	Shakespeare, William	(collection) 1623	1611	22273
391	The Two Gentlemen of Verona	Shakespeare, William	(collection) 1623	1593	22273
392	Measure for Measure	Shakespeare, William	(collection) 1623	1604	22273
393	The Comedy of Errors	Shakespeare, William	(collection) 1623	1592	22273
394	As you Like it	Shakespeare, William	(collection) 1623	1599	22273
395	All's Well that Ends Well	Shakespeare, William	(collection) 1623	1602	22273
396	Twelfth Night or What you Will	Shakespeare, William	(collection) 1623	1600	22273
397	The Winter's Tale	Shakespeare, William	(collection) 1623	1610	22273
398	King John	Shakespeare, William	(collection) 1623	1596	22273

GREG #	PLAY	AUTHOR	GREG DATE	H-S DATE	STC
399	1 Henry the Sixth	Shakespeare, William	(collection) 1623	1592	22273
400	Henry the Eighth	Shakespeare, W. (& Fletcher, J.?)	(collection) 1623	1613	22273
401	Coriolanus	Shakespeare, William	(collection) 1623	1608	22273
402	Timon of Athens	Shakespeare, William	(collection) 1623	1607	22273
403	Julius Caesar	Shakespeare, William	(collection) 1623	1599	22273
404	Macbeth	Shakespeare, William	(collection) 1623	1606	22273
405	Antony and Cleopatra	Shakespeare, William	(collection) 1623	1607	22273
406	Cymbeline	Shakespeare, William	(collection) 1623	1609	22273
407	Neptune's Triumph	Jonson, Ben	6 Jan. 1624	1624	14779
408	The Bondman	Massinger, Philip	12 Mar. 1624	1623	17632
409	Monuments of Honour	Webster, John	29 Oct. 1624	1624	25175
410	Nero (Piso's Conspiracy)	Anon.	1624	1624	18430
411	The Fortunate Isles	Jonson, Ben	6 Jan. 1625	1625	14772

GREG #	PLAY	AUTHOR	GREG DATE	H-S DATE	STC
412	A Game at Chess	Middleton, Thomas	? 1625	1624	17882
413	The Triumphs of Health and Prosperity	Middleton, Thomas	30 Oct. 1626	1626	17898
414	Apollo Shroving	Hawkins, William	(after 25 Apr.) 1627	1627	12963
415	The Andrian Woman	Newman, Thomas	(collection) 1627	1627	23897
416	The Eunuch	Newman, Thomas	(collection) 1627	1627	23897
417	Aminta	Reynolds, Henry	(7 Nov. 1627) 1628	1628	23696
418	Lodovick Sforza	Gomersall, Robert	27 Feb. 1628	1628	11995
419	Britannia's Honour	Dekker, Thomas	29 Oct. 1628	1628	6493
420	The Lover's Melancholy	Ford, John	2 June 1629	1628	11163
421	London's Tempe	Dekker, Thomas	29 Oct. 1629	1629	6509
422	Albovine	Davenant, William	1629	1628	6307
423	The Deserving Favourite	Carlell, Lodowick	1629	1629	4628
424	The Roman Actor	Massinger, Philip	1629	1626	17642

GREG #	PLAY	AUTHOR	GREG DATE	H-S DATE	STC
425	The Wedding	Shirley, James	1629	1626	22460
426	Wine, Beer, Ale, and Tobacco (Wine, Beer, and Ale)	Anon.	1629	1625	11541
427	The Cruel Brother	Davenant, William	10 Jan. 1630	1627	6302
428	The Just Italian	Davenant, William	10 Jan. 1630	1629	6303
429	The Grateful Servant	Shirley, James	26 Feb. 1630	1629	22444
430	The Renegado	Massinger, Philip	22 Mar. 1630	1624	17641
431	Aristippus	Randolph, Thomas	26 Mar. 1630	1626	20686
432	The Conceited Pedlar	Randolph, Thomas	26 Mar. 1630	1627	20686
433	A Chaste Maid in Cheapside	Middleton, Thomas	8 Apr. 1630	1613	17877
434	Pathomachia	Anon.	16 Apr. 1630	1617	19462
435	2 The Honest Whore	Dekker, Thomas	29 June 1630	1605	6506
436	The Picture	Massinger, Philip	1630	1629	17640
437	Love's Triumph through Callipolis	Jonson, Ben	(9 Jan.–24 Mar. 1631) 1630	1631	14776

GREG #	PLAY	AUTHOR	GREG DATE	H-S DATE	STC
438.	Hoffman	Chettle, Henry	(26 Feb. 1630) 1631	1602	5125
439	The Spanish Bawd	Mabbe, James	(27 Feb. 1630) 1631	1631	4911
440	Match me in London	Dekker, Thomas	(8 Nov. 1630) 1631	1611	6529
441	The School of Compliment (Love Tricks)	Shirley, James	25 Feb. 1631	1625	22456
442	The New Inn	Jonson, Ben	17 Apr. 1631	1629	14780
443	Sicelides	Fletcher, Phineas	25 Apr. 1631	1615	11083
444	Caesar and Pompey	Chapman, George	18 May 1631	1605	4993
445	1 The Fair Maid of the West	Heywood, Thomas	16 June 1631	1610	13320
446	2 The Fair Maid of the West	Heywood, Thomas	16 June 1631	1631	13320
447	The Raging Turk	Goffe, Thomas	7 Sept. 1631	1618	11980
448	London's Ius Honorarium	Heywood, Thomas	29 Oct. 1631	1631	13351
449	Rhodon and Iris	Knevet, Ralph	12 Nov. 1631	1631	15036
450	Antigone	May, Thomas	1631	1627	17716
451	The Duchess of Suffolk	Drue, Thomas	1631	1624	7242

GREG #	PLAY	AUTHOR	GREG DATE	H-S DATE	STC
452.	Chloridia	Jonson, Ben	(after 22 Feb.) 1631	1631	14762
453	Albion's Triumph	Townshend, Aurelian	(8 Jan.–24 Mar. 1632) 1631	1632	24155
454	Tempe Restored	Townshend, Aurelian	(14 Feb.–24 Mar. 1632) 1631	1632	24156
455	Bartholmew Fair	Jonson, Ben	(collection) 1631	1614	14754
456	The Staple of News	Jonson, Ben	(collection) 1631	1626	14754
457	The Devil is an Ass	Jonson, Ben	(collection) 1631	1616	14754
458	The Courageous Turk	Goffe, Thomas	(7 Sept. 1631) 1632	1618	11977
459	The Emperor of the East	Massinger, Philip	(19 Nov. 1631) 1632	1631	17636
460	A New Wonder, a Woman never Vexed	Rowley, William	(24 Nov. 1631) 1632	1625	21423
461	Holland's Leaguer	Marmion, Shackerly	26 Jan. 1632	1631	17443
462	Changes	Shirley, James	9 Feb. 1632	1632	

GREG #	PLAY	AUTHOR	GREG DATE	H-S DATE	STC
463	The Northern Lass	Brome, Richard	24 Mar. 1632	1629	3819
464	The Fatal Dowry	Field, N.; Massinger, P.	30 Mar. 1632	1619	17646
465	The Rival Friends	Hausted, Peter	13 June 1632	1632	12935
466	Londini Scaturigo	Heywood, Thomas	29 Oct. 1632	1632	13347
467	1 The Iron Age	Heywood, Thomas	1632	1612	13340
468	2 The Iron Age	Heywood, Thomas	1632	1612	13340
469	The Jealous Lovers	Randolph, Thomas	1632	1632	20692
470	The Maid of Honour	Massinger, Philip	1632	1621	17638
471	All's Lost by Lust	Rowley, William	(27 Sept. 1632) 1633	1619	21425
472	The Costly Whore	Anon.	(2 Nov. 1632) 1633	1620	25582
473	Honoria and Mammon (A Contention for Honour and Riches)	Shirley, James	(9 Nov. 1632) 1633	1631	22439
474	A New Way to Pay Old Debts	Massinger, Philip	(10 Nov. 1632) 1633	1625	17639

	PLAY	AUTHOR	GREG DATE	H-S DATE	STC
475	The Jew of Malta	Marlowe, C. (revised by Heywood, T., c. 1632?)	(20 Nov. 1632) 1633	1589	17412
476	A Match at Midnight	Rowley, W. (& Middleton, T.?)	15 Jan. 1633	1622	21421
477	The Witty Fair One	Shirley, James	15 Jan. 1633	1628	22462
478	Love's Sacrifice	Ford, John	21 Jan. 1633	1632	11164
479	The Bird in a Cage	Shirley, James	19 Mar. 1633	1633	22436
480	The Broken Heart	Ford, John	28 Mar. 1633	1629	11156
481	A Fine Companion	Marmion, Shackerly	15 June 1633	1633	17442
482	Fuimus Troes	Fisher, Jasper	1 Aug. 1633	1626	10886
483	Londini Emporia	Heywood, Thomas	29 Oct. 1633	1633	13348
484	The English Traveller	Heywood, Thomas	1633	1625	13315
485	Orestes	Goffe, Thomas	1633	1617	11982
486	'Tis Pity she's a Whore	Ford, John	1633	1632	11165
487	The Entertainment at Edinburgh	Drummond, William (?)	(after 15 June) 1633	1633	5023

GREG #	PLAY	AUTHOR	GREG DATE	H-S DATE	STC
488	The Triumph of Peace	Shirley, James	(3 Feb.–24 Mar. 1634) 1633	1634	22459
489	Alaham	Greville, Fulke	(collection) 1633	1600	12361
490	The Noble Soldier	Dekker, T. ('S. R.' [Samuel Rowley?] on t.p.)	(9 Dec. 1633) 1634	1626	21416
491	Perkin Warbeck	Ford, J. (& Dekker, T.?)	24 Feb. 1634	1633	11157
492	The Two Noble Kinsmen	'John Fletcher and William Shakespeare' (Shakespeare's sole authorship recently urged)	8 Apr. 1634	1613	11075
493	A Maidenhead well Lost	Heywood, Thomas	25 June 1634	1633	13357
494	The Late Lancashire Witches	Brome, R.; Heywood, T.	28 Oct. 1634	1634	13373
495	The Triumphs of Fame and Honour	Taylor, John	29 Oct. 1634	1634	23808

GREG #	PLAY	AUTHOR	GREG DATE	H-S DATE	STC
496	Coelum Britannicum	Carew, Thomas	(after 24 Mar.) 1634	1634	4618
497	The Temple of Love	Davenant, William	(10 Feb.–24 Mar. 1635) 1634	1635	14719
498	The Traitor	Shirley, James	(3 Nov. 1634) 1635	1631	22458
499	The Shepherds' Holiday	Rutter, Joseph	19 Jan. 1635	1634	21470
500	Londini Sinus Salutis	Heywood, Thomas	29 Oct. 1635	1635	13348a
501	Adrasta	Jones, John	1635	1635	14721
502	The Triumphs of the Price d'Amour	Davenant, William	(24 Feb.–24 Mar. 1636) 1635	1636	6308
503	Corona Mineruae	Kynaston, Francis (?)	(27 Feb.–24 Mar. 1636) 1635	1636	15100
504	Love's Mistress	Heywood, Thomas	(30 Sept. 1635) 1636	1634	13352
505	The Great Duke of Florence	Massinger, Philip	(7 Dec. 1635) 1636	1627	17637

GREG #	PLAY	AUTHOR	GREG DATE	H-S DATE	STC
506	The Platonic Lovers	Davenant, William	4 Feb. 1636	1635	6305
507	The Wits	Davenant, William	4 Feb. 1636	1634	6309
508	The Wonder of a Kingdom	Dekker, T. (& Day, J.?)	24 Feb. 1636	1631	6533
509	A Challenge for Beauty	Heywood, Thomas	17 June 1636	1635	13311
510	The Vow Breaker	Sampson, William	1636	1625	21688
511	The Presentment of Bushell's Rock	Anon.	(after 23 Aug.) 1636	1636	4188
512	The Entertainment at Richmond	Sackville, E. (?); & others	(after 12 Sept.) 1636	1636	5026
513	Hannibal and Scipio	Nabbes, Thomas	(6 Aug. 1636) 1637	1635	18341
514	Microcosmus	Nabbes, Thomas	(6 Aug. 1636) 1637	1637	18342
515	The Elder Brother	Fletcher, J. (revised by Massinger?)	24 Mar. 1637	1625	11066
516	The Royal King and the Loyal Subject	Heywood, T. (& Smith, Went.?)	25 Mar. 1637	1602	13364
517	Hyde Park	Shirley, James	13 Apr. 1637	1632	22446

GREG #	PLAY	AUTHOR	GREG DATE	H-S DATE	STC
518	The Lady of Pleasure	Shirley, James	13 Apr. 1637	1635	22448
519	The Young Admiral	Shirley, James	13 Apr. 1637	1633	22463
520	The Valiant Scot	'J.W.'	26 Apr. 1637	1637	24910
521	The Example	Shirley, James	18 Oct. 1637	1634	22442
522	Londini Speculum	Heywood, Thomas	30 Oct. 1637	1637	13349
523	The Gamester	Shirley, James	15 Nov. 1637	1633	22443
524	The Masque at Ludlow Castle [Comus]	Milton, John	1637	1634	17937
525	1 The Cid	Rutter, J. (with Sackville, E. & R.?)	(29 Jan. 1638) 1637	1637	5770
526	Britannia Triumphans	Davenant, William	(8 Jan.–24 Mar. 1638) 1637	1638	14718
527	Luminalia	Davenant, William	(6 Feb.–24 Mar. 1638) 1637	1638	16923
528	Jupiter and Io	Heywood, Thomas	(collection) 1637	1635	13358
529	Apollo and Daphne	Heywood, Thomas	(collection) 1637	1635	13358

GREG #	PLAY	AUTHOR	GREG DATE	H-S DATE	STC
530	Amphrisa	Heywood, Thomas	(collection) 1637	1635	13358
531	A Shoemaker a Gentleman	Rowley, William	(28 Nov. 1637) 1638	1608	21422
532	The Fancies	Ford, John	3 Feb. 1638	1635	11159
533	The Martyred Soldier	Shirley, H. (& Heywood, T.?)	15 Feb. 1638	1618	22435
534	The Lost Lady	Berkeley, William	5 Mar. 1638	1637	1902
535	The Wise Woman of Hogsdon	Heywood, Thomas	12 Mar. 1638	1604	13370
536	The Duke's Mistress	Shirley, James	13 Mar. 1638	1636	22441
537	Paliantus and Eudora (The Conspiracy)	Killigrew, Henry	13 Mar. 1638	1635	14958
538	The Royal Master	Shirley, James	13 Mar. 1638	1637	22454
539	Love's Riddle	Cowley, Abraham	14 Mar. 1638	1633	5904
540	Tottenham Court	Nabbes, Thomas	5 Apr. 1638	1634	18344
541	Aglaura	Suckling, John	18 Apr. 1638	1637	23420
542	Covent Garden	Nabbes, Thomas	28 May 1638	1633	18339
543	The Spring's Glory	Nabbes, Thomas	23 June 1638	1637	18343

GREG #	PLAY	AUTHOR	GREG DATE	H-S DATE	STC
544	The Presentation for the Prince [Time and the Almanac-Makers]	Nabbes, Thomas	23 June 1638	1638	18343
545	The Seven Champions of Christendom	Kirke, John	13 July 1638	1635	15014
546	Porta Pietatis	Heywood, Thomas	29 Oct. 1638	1638	13359
547	The Muses' Looking-Glass	Randolph, Thomas	(collection) 1638	1630	20694
548	Amyntas	Randolph, Thomas	(collection) 1638	1630	20694
549	The Ball	Shirley, James	(24 Oct. 1638) 1639	1632	4995
550	Chabot Admiral of France	Chapman, George	(24 Oct. 1638) 1639	1622	4996
551	1 Arviragus and Philicia	Carlell, Lodowick	(26 Oct. 1638) 1639	1636	4627
552	2 Arviragus and Philicia	Carlell, Lodowick	(26 Oct. 1638) 1639	1636	4627
553	Cleopatra	May, Thomas	(26 Oct. 1638) 1639	1626	17717
554	Julia Agrippina	May, Thomas	(26 Oct. 1638) 1639	1628	17718
555	The Lady's Trial	Ford, John	(6 Nov. 1638) 1639	1638	11161
556	The Sophister	Zouche, Richard	(7 Nov. 1638) 1639	1631	26133

GREG #	PLAY	AUTHOR	GREG DATE	H-S DATE	STC
557	Argalus and Parthenia	Glapthorne, Henry	11 Jan. 1639	1638	11908
558	Monsieur Thomas (Father's own Son)	Fletcher, John	22 Jan. 1639	1615	11071
559	The Unnatural Combat	Massinger, Philip	14 Feb. 1639	1626	17643
560	Imperiale	Freeman, Ralph	1 Mar. 1639	1639	11369
561	A New Trick to Cheat the Devil	Davenport, Robert	28 Mar. 1639	1625	6315
562	The Maid's Revenge	Shirley, James	12 Apr. 1639	1626	22450
563	Wit without Money	Fletcher, J. (revised by another?)	25 Apr. 1639	1614	1691
564	Albertus Wallenstein	Glapthorne, Henry	22 Sept. 1639	1634	11912
565	Rollo Duke of Normandy (The Bloody Brother)	Fletcher (with Massinger?; Jonson?; & another?)	4 Oct. 1639	1619	11064
566	Londini Status Pacatus	Heywood, Thomas	29 Oct. 1639	1639	13350
567	The Bloody Banquet	'T.D.' (Drue, Thomas?)	1639	1639	6181
568	The City Match	Mayne, Jasper	1639	1637	17750
569	The Phoenix in her Flames	Lower, William	1639	1639	16873

GREG #	PLAY	AUTHOR	GREG DATE	H-S DATE	STC
570	The Royal Slave	Cartwright, William	1639	1636	4717
571	Salmacida Spolia	Davenant, William	(21 Jan.–24 Mar. 1640) 1639	1640	6306
572	The Coronation	Shirley, James	(25 Apr. 1639) 1640	1635	22440
573	Love's Cruelty	Shirley, James	(25 Apr. 1639) 1640	1631	22449
574	The Night Walker	Fletcher, John	(25 Apr. 1639) 1640	1611	11072
575	The Opportunity	Shirley, James	(25 Apr. 1639) 1640	1634	22451
576	The Bride	Nabbes, Thomas	(8 July 1639) 1640	1638	18338
577	The Humorous Courtier	Shirley, James	(29 July 1639) 1640	1631	22447
578	Messalina	Richards, Nathaniel	(3 Oct. 1639) 1640	1635	21011
579	Christ's Passion	Sandys, George	(9 Oct. 1639) 1640	1640	12397
580	The Knave in Grain	'J.D.' (author or reviser?)	(22 Oct. 1639) 1640	1639	6174

GREG #	PLAY	AUTHOR	GREG DATE	H-S DATE	STC
581	The Unfortunate Mother	Nabbes, Thomas	(4 Nov. 1639) 1640	1639	18346
582	The Rebellion	Rawlins, Thomas	(20 Nov. 1639) 1640	1636	20770
583	The Arcadia	Shirley, James (?)	(29 Nov. 1639) 1640	1640	22453
584	The Strange Discovery	Gough, John	31 Jan. 1640	1640	12133
585	The Gipsies Metamorphosed	Jonson, Ben	20 Feb. 1640	1621	14777a
586	The Antipodes	Brome, Richard	19 Mar. 1640	1638	3818
587	The Sparagus Garden	Brome, Richard	19 Mar. 1640	1635	3820
588	The Queen of Aragon	Habington, William	2 Apr. 1640	1640	12587
589	The Swaggering Damsel	Chamberlain, Robert	2 Apr. 1640	1640	4946
590	The Ladies' Privilege	Glapthorne, Henry	4 Apr. 1640	1637	11910
591	Wit in a Constable	Glapthorne, Henry	27 Apr. 1640	1638	11914
592	The Constant Maid (Love will Find out the Way)	Shirley, James	28 Apr. 1640	1638	22438
593	1 Saint Patrick for Ireland	Shirley, James	28 Apr. 1640	1639	22455
594	The Hollander	Glapthorne, Henry	22 May 1640	1636	11909

GREG #	PLAY	AUTHOR	GREG DATE	H-S DATE	STC
595	Mascarade du Ciel	Sadler, John	24 Nov. 1640	1640	21542
596	2 The Cid	Rutter, J. (with Sackville, E. & R.?)	1640	1638	5771
597	The Noble Stranger	Sharpe, Lewis	1640	1639	22377
598	Rule a Wife and Have a Wife	Fletcher, John	1640	1624	11073
599	Sicily and Naples	Harding, Samuel	1640	1640	12757
600	Love Crowns the End	Tatham, John	(collection) 1640	1632	23704
601	The Antiquary	Marmion, Shack-erly	(11 Mar. 1640) 1641	1635	M703
602	The Parliament of Bees	Day, John	23 Mar. 1641	1640	D466
603	Canterbury his Change of Diet	Anon.	1641	1641	C454
604	Landgartha	Burnell, Henry	1641	1640	B5751
605	Mercurius Britannicus	Brathwait, Richard	(after 12 May) 1641	1641	B4270
606	Christmas his Masque	Jonson, Ben	(collection) 1641	1616	14754
607	The Vision of Delight	Jonson, Ben	(collection) 1641	1617	14754
608	Pleasure Reconciled to Virtue	Jonson, Ben	(collection) 1641	1618	14754

GREG #	PLAY	AUTHOR	GREG DATE	H-S DATE	STC
609	For the Honour of Wales	Jonson, Ben	(collection) 1641	1618	14754
610	News from the New World Discovered in the Moon	Jonson, Ben	(collection) 1641	1620	14754
611	Pan's Anniversary	Jonson, Ben	(collection) 1641	1620	14754
612	The Masque of Owls	Jonson, Ben	(collection) 1641	1624	14754
613	The Entertainment at Welbeck [Love's Welcome at Welbeck]	Jonson, Ben	(collection) 1641	1633	14754
614	Love's Welcome [at Bolsover]	Jonson, Ben	(collection) 1641	1634	14754
615	Mortimer his Fall	Jonson, Ben	(collection) 1641	1637	14754
616	The Magnetic Lady	Jonson, Ben	(collection) 1641	1632	14754
617	A Tale of a Tub	Jonson, Ben	(collection) 1641	1596/ 1633	14754
618	The Sad Shepherd	Jonson, Ben	(collection) 1641	1637	14754
619	The Prisoners	Killigrew, Thomas	(collection) 1641	1635	14959/ K452
620	Claricilla (Claracilla)	Killigrew, Thomas	(collection) 1641	1636	14959/ K452

GREG #	PLAY	GREG DATE	AUTHOR	H-S DATE	STC
621	Brennoralt (The Discontented Colonel)	5 Apr. 1642	Suckling, John	1639	S6125
622	The Sophy	6 Aug. 1642	Denham, John	1641	D1009
623	Tyrannical Government Anatomized	(30 Jan.–24 Mar. 1643) 1642	Anon.	1643	B5298
624	The Unfortunate Lovers	1643	Davenant, William	1638	D348
625	Arcades	(collection) 1645	Milton, John	1633	M2160
626	Cola's Fury	1646	Burkhead, Henry	1645	B5734
627	The Triumph of Beauty	(collection) 1646	Shirley, James	1646	S3488
628	The Goblins	(collection) 1646	Suckling, John	1638	S6126
629	Il Pastor Fido	8 June 1647	Fanshawe, Richard	1647	G2174
630	1 The Committee-Man Curried	1647	Sheppard, Samuel	1647	S3160
631	2 The Committee-Man Curried	1647	Sheppard, Samuel	1647	S3168

GREG #	PLAY	AUTHOR	GREG DATE	H-S DATE	STC
632	The Country Girl	'T.B.' (Brewer, Anth. or Th.?)	1647	1632	B4425
633	Gripus and Hegio	Baron, Robert	1647	1647	B889
634	Deorum Dona	Baron, Robert	1647	1647	B889
635	The Levellers Levelled	Nedham, Marchmont	1647	1647	N394
635.5	News out of the West	Anon.	1647	1647	N1036a
636	The Scottish Politic Presbyter	Anon.	1647	1647	S2097
637	The Mad Lover	Fletcher, John	(collection) 1647	1617	B1581
638	The Spanish Curate	Fletcher, J.; Massinger, P.	(collection) 1647	1622	B1581
639	The Little French Lawyer	Fletcher, J.; Massinger, P.	(collection) 1647	1619	B1581
640	The Custom of the Country	Fletcher, J.; Massinger, P.	(collection) 1647	1620	B1581
641	The Noble Gentleman	Fletcher (poss. completed or revised by another)	(collection) 1647	1626	B1581

GREG #	PLAY	AUTHOR	GREG DATE	H-S DATE	STC
642	The Captain	Fletcher, J. (with Beaumont, F.?)	(collection) 1647	1612	B1581
643	Beggars' Bush	Fletcher, J. (with Massinger, P.?)	(collection) 1647	1622	B1581
644	The Coxcomb	Fletcher, with Beaumont (revised by Massinger or Rowley, W.?)	(collection) 1647	1609	B1581
645	The False One	Fletcher, J.; Massinger, P.	(collection) 1647	1620	B1581
646	The Chances	Fletcher, John	(collection) 1647	1625	B1581
647	The Loyal Subject	Fletcher, John	(collection) 1647	1618	B1581
648	The Laws of Candy	Fletcher, J. (revised by another?)	(collection) 1647	1619	B1581
649	The Lover's Progress	Fletcher, J. (& Massinger, P.?)	(collection) 1647	1623	B1581

GREG #	PLAY	AUTHOR	GREG DATE	H-S DATE	STC
650	The Island Princess	Fletcher, John	(collection) 1647	1621	B1581
651	The Humorous Lieutenant	Fletcher, John	(collection) 1647	1619	B1581
652	The Nice Valour	Fletcher (revised by Middleton or another?)	(collection) 1647	1616	B1581
653	The Maid in the Mill	Fletcher, J.; Rowley, W.	(collection) 1647	1623	B1581
654	The Prophetess	Fletcher, John; Massinger, P.	(collection) 1647	1622	B1581
655	Bonduca	Fletcher, John	(collection) 1647	1613	B1581
656	The Sea Voyage	Fletcher, J.; Massinger, P.	(collection) 1647	1622	B1581
657	The Double Marriage	Fletcher, J.; Massinger, P.	(collection) 1647	1620	B1581
658	The Pilgrim	Fletcher, John	(collection) 1647	1621	B1581
659	The Knight of Malta	Fletcher; Field; Massinger	(collection) 1647	1618	B1581

GREG #	PLAY	AUTHOR	GREG DATE	H-S DATE	STC
660	The Woman's Prize	Fletcher, John	(collection) 1647	1611	B1581
661	Love's Cure	Massinger (revising Beaumont & Fletcher?)	(collection) 1647	1625	B1581
662	The Honest Man's Fortune	Fletcher (with Field? Massinger? Tourneur?)	(collection) 1647	1613	B1581
663	The Queen of Corinth	Fletcher (& Massinger? Field?)	(collection) 1647	1617	B1581
664	Women Pleased	Fletcher, John	(collection) 1647	1620	B1581
665	A Wife for a Month	Fletcher, John	(collection) 1647	1624	B1581
666	Wit at Several Weapons	Fletcher, J. (with Middleton? Rowley, W.?)	(collection) 1647	1609	B1581
667	Valentinian	Fletcher, John	(collection) 1647	1614	B1581

GREG #	PLAY	AUTHOR	GREG DATE	H-S DATE	STC
668	The Fair Maid of the Inn	Fletcher (with Massinger? Rowley, W.? & Ford?)	(collection) 1647	1626	B1581
669	Love's Pilgrimage	Fletcher, J. (with Beaumont, F.?)	(collection) 1647	1616	B1581
670	Four Plays in One	Fletcher, J. (with Beaumont? or Field?)	(collection) 1647	1612	B1581
671	The Amorous War	Mayne, Jasper	1648	1638	M1463
672	1 Crafty Cromwell	Anon.	1648	1648	C6772
673	2 Crafty Cromwell	Anon.	1648	1648	S2294
673.5	The Devil and the Parliament	Anon.	1648	1648	D1216
674	Ding-Dong	Anon.	1648	1648	D1495
674.5	The Kentish Fair	Anon.	1648	1648	K324
675	Medea	Sherburne, Edward	1648	1648	S2513
676	Mistress Parliament Brought to Bed	Anon.	1648	1648	M2281
677	Mistress Parliament Presented in her Bed	Anon.	1648	1648	M2284
678	Mistress Parliament her Gossiping	Anon.	1648	1648	M2282
678.5	Mistress Parliament her Invitation of Mistress London	Anon.	1648	1648	M2283

GREG #	PLAY	AUTHOR	GREG DATE	H-S DATE	STC
679	A Bartholmew Fairing	Anon.	1649	1649	B981
680	Charles the First	Anon.	(after 29 Jan.) 1649	1649	F384
681	The Country Captain	Cavendish, W.; Shirley, J.	1649	1640	N877
682	The Disease of the House	Anon.	1649	1649	D1667
683	Electra	Wase, Christopher	1649	1649	S4690
684	Love and Honour	Davenant, William	1649	1634	D329
685	Love in its Ecstasy	Peaps, [William?](?)	1649	1634	P967
686	A New Bull-Baiting	Anon.	1649	1649	N587
687	1 Newmarket Fair	Anon.	1649	1649	T2018
688	2 Newmarket Fair	Anon.	1649	1649	S2318
689	The Rebellion of Naples	'T.B.'	1649	1649	B199
690	The Virgin Widow	Quarles, Francis	1649	1641	Q118
691	Women will have their Will	Anon.	1649	1649	W3327
692	The Variety	Cavendish, W. (& Shirley, J.?)	(collection) 1649	1641	N877

GREG #	PLAY	AUTHOR	GREG DATE	H-S DATE	STC
693	The Guardian (Cutter of Coleman Street)	Cowley, Abraham	1650	1642	C6673
694	The Distracted State	Tatham, John	(23 Nov. 1650) 1651	1650	T219
695	Astraea	Willan, Leonard	1651	1651	W2262
696	Hippolytus	Prestwich, Edmund	1651	1651	S2512
697	The Jovial Crew [or The Devil Turned Ranter]	Sheppard, Samuel	1651	1651	S3166
698	Marcus Tullius Cicero	Anon.	1651	1651	B4902
699	Πλουτοφθαλμία Πλουτογαμία	Randolph, T. (revised by 'F.J.')	1651	1627	A3685
700	The Prince of Prigs' Revels	'J.S.'	1651	1651	S58
701	The Lady Errant	Cartwright, William	(collection) 1651	1637	C709
702	The Ordinary	Cartwright, William	(collection) 1651	1635	C709
703	The Siege	Cartwright, William	(collection) 1651	1638	C709
704	The Just General	Manuche, Cosmo	(29 Nov. 1651) 1652	1652	M549

GREG #	PLAY	AUTHOR	GREG DATE	H-S DATE	STC
705	The Widow	Middleton (with 'Ben Jonson. John Fletcher'?)	12 Apr. 1652	1616	J1015
706	The Wild-Goose Chase	Fletcher, John	12 Apr. 1652	1621	B1616
707	The Bastard	Anon. (prob. not Manuche, C.)	1652	1652	M548
708	A Jovial Crew [or The Merry Beggars]	Brome, Richard	1652	1641	B4873
709	The Loyal Lovers	Manuche, Cosmo	1652	1652	M550
710	Sophompaneas	Goldsmith, Francis	1652	1652	G2125
711	The Scots Figgaries	Tatham, John	1652	1652	T235
712	The Changeling	Middleton, T.; Rowley, W.	(19 Oct. 1652) 1653	1622	M1981
713	Cupid and Death	Shirley, James	(before 16 Nov.) 1653	1653	S3464
714	The Fatal Contract (The Eunuch)	Hemming, William	1653	1639	H1422
715	The Ghost	Anon.	1653	1640	G641
716	The Queen	Ford, John(?)	1653	1628	Q155

GREG #	PLAY	AUTHOR	GREG DATE	H-S DATE	STC
717	The Spanish Gipsy	Middleton; Rowley, W. (Ford sometimes urged as part-author)	1653	1623	M1986
718	A Mad Couple well Matched	Brome, Richard	(collection) 1653	1639	B4870
719	The Novella	Brome, Richard	(collection) 1653	1632	B4870
720	The Court Beggar	Brome, Richard	(collection) 1653	1640	B4870
721	The City Wit	Brome, Richard	(collection) 1653	1630	B4870
722	The Damoiselle	Brome, Richard	(collection) 1653	1638	B4870
723	The Brothers	Shirley, James	(collection) 1653	1641	S3486
724	The Sisters	Shirley, James	(collection) 1653	1642	S3486
725	The Doubtful Heir	Shirley, James	(collection) 1653	1638	S3486
726	The Imposture	Shirley, James	(collection) 1653	1640	S3486

GREG #	PLAY	AUTHOR	GREG DATE	H-S DATE	STC
727	The Cardinal	Shirley, James	(collection) 1653	1641	S3486
728	The Court Secret	Shirley, James	(collection) 1653	1642	S3486
729	Alphonsus of Germany	Anon. (Peele, G.?)	(9 Sept. 1653) 1654	1594	C1952
730	Revenge for Honour	Glapthorne (?) ('George Chapman' on t.p., 'Henry Glapthorne' in S.R. Glapthorne prob. author rather than reviser.)	(29 Dec. 1653) 1654	1640	C1949
731	The Nuptials of Peleus and Thetis	Howell, James	28 Apr. 1654	1654	H3097
732	The Nuptials of Peleus and Thetis	Howell, James	28 Apr. 1654	1654	H3097
733	Appius and Virginia	Webster, J. (& Heywood, T.?)	13 May 1654	1624	W1216
734	Ariadne	Flecknoe, Richard	1654	1654	F1209
735	The Combat of Love and Friendship	Mead, Robert	1654	1638	M1564

GREG #	PLAY	AUTHOR	GREG DATE	H-S DATE	STC
736	The Cunning Lovers	Brome, Alexander(?)	1654	1638	B4850
737	The Extravagant Shepherd	'T.R.'	1654	1654	C6323
738	Love's Dominion (Love's Kingdom)	Flecknoe, Richard	1654	1654	F1228
739	Fortune by Land and Sea	Heywood, T.; Rowley, W.	20 June 1655	1609	H1783
740	The Lovesick King	Brewer, Anthony	20 June 1655	1617	B4426
741	The Poor Man's Comfort	Daborne, Robert	20 June 1655	1617	D101
742	The Twins	Rider, William	20 June 1655	1635	R1446
743	The Clouds	Stanley, Thomas	16 Aug. 1655	1655	S5237
744	Mirza	Baron, Robert	16 Aug. 1655	1655	B891
745	Filli di Sciro	Sidnam, Jonathan	1655	1630	B3554
746	The Floating Island	Strode, William	1655	1636	S5983
747	The Gentleman of Venice	Shirley, James	1655	1639	S3469
748	The Gossips' Brawl	Anon.	1655	1655	G1315
749	King John and Matilda	Davenport, Robert	1655	1631	D370

GREG #	PLAY	AUTHOR	GREG DATE	H-S DATE	STC
750	1 The Passionate Lover	Carlell, Lodowick	1655	1638	C581
751	2 The Passionate Lover	Carlell, Lodowick	1655	1638	C581
752	The Politician	Shirley, James	1655	1639	S3483
753	Polyeuctes	Lower, William	1655	1655	C6316
754	Actaeon and Diana	Cox, Robert (author or adapter)	(collection) 1655	1653	C6710
755	Singing Simpkin (Simpkin)	Kempe, William(?)	(collection) 1655	1595	C6710
756	Oenone	Cox, Robert (author or adapter)	(collection) 1655	1653	C6710
757	John Swabber	Cox, Robert (author or adapter)	(collection) 1655	1653	C6710
758	The Bashful Lover	Massinger, Philip	(collection) 1655	1636	M1050
759	The Guardian	Massinger, Philip	(collection) 1655	1633	M1050
760	A Very Woman	Massinger, Philip (reviser)	(collection) 1655	1634	M1050

GREG #	PLAY	AUTHOR	GREG DATE	H-S DATE	STC
761	The Careless Shepherdess	Goffe, Thomas (?)	(22 Oct. 1655) 1656	1619	G1005
762	The Hectors	Anon. (wrongly assigned to Prestwich, E.)	(22 Oct. 1655) 1656	1656	P3315
763	1 The Siege of Rhodes	Davenant, William	27 Aug. 1656	1656	D339
764	London's Triumph for Robert Tichborne	'I.B.' (Bulteel, John?)	29 Oct. 1656	1656	B5455
765	Horatius	Lower, William	1656	1656	·C6313
766	The Old Law	Middleton; Rowley, W.; Massinger	1656	1618	M1048
767	The Sun's Darling	Dekker, T.; Ford, J.	1656	1624	F1467
768	Venus and Adonis	Holland, Samuel	1656	1656	H2437
769	Simpleton the Smith	Cox, Robert (author or adapter)	(collection) 1656	1653	C6711
770	The Entertainment at Rutland House	Davenant, William	(9 Sept. 1656) 1657	1656	D323
771	The Obstinate Lady	Cokain, Aston	(29 Sept. 1656) 1657	1639	C4896

GREG #	PLAY	AUTHOR	GREG DATE	H-S DATE	STC
772	The Queen's Exchange (The Royal Exchange)	Brome, Richard	(20 Nov. 1656) 1657	1631	B4882
773	The Walks of Islington and Hogsdon (Tricks of Youth)	Jordan, Thomas	21 Apr. 1657	1641	J1071
774	The False Favourite Disgraced	D'Ouvilley, George Gerbier	16 June 1657	1657	G584
775	London's Triumphs for Richard Chiverton	Tatham, John	29 Oct. 1657	1657	T226
776	Fancy's Festivals	Jordan, Thomas	1657	1657	J1031
777	Lust's Dominion	Anon. ('Christopher Marlowe' on t.p.; by Day; Dekker; Haughton? [& Marston?])	1657	1600	L3504a
778	No Wit like a Woman's	Middleton, Thomas	1657	1612	M1985
779	The Fool would be a Favourite	Carlell, Lodowick	(collection) 1657	1637	C582
780	Osmond the Great Turk	Carlell, Lodowick	(collection) 1657	1637	C582
781	More Dissemblers besides Women	Middleton, Thomas	(collection) 1657	1615	M1989

GREG #	PLAY	AUTHOR	GREG DATE	H-S DATE	STC
782	Women Beware Women	Middleton, Thomas	(collection) 1657	1621	M1989
783	Orgula	Willan, Leonard	(24 Apr. 1657) 1658	1658	W2264
784	The Old Couple	May, Thomas	7 Jan. 1658	1636	M1412
785	The Witch of Edmonton	Dekker; Ford; Rowley, W.	21 May 1658	1621	R2097
786	London's Triumph for John Ireton	Tatham, John	29 Oct. 1658	1658	T225
787	The Cruelty of the Spaniards in Peru	Davenant, William	30 Nov. 1658	1658	D321
788	The City Madam	Massinger, Philip	1658	1632	M1046
789	The Contention of Ajax and Ulisses	Shirley, James	1658	1658	S3475
790	The Enchanted Lovers	Lower, William	1658	1658	L3314
791	Love and War	Meriton, Thomas	1658	1658	M1822
792	Love's Victory	Chamberlaine, William	1658	1658	C1865
793	The Unhappy Fair Irene	Swinhoe, Gilbert	1658	1658	S6263
794	The Wandering Lover	Meriton, Thomas	1658	1658	M1824

GREG #	PLAY	AUTHOR	GREG DATE	H-S DATE	STC
795	The Masque at Bretby	Cokain, Aston	(collection) 1658	1640	C4894
796	Trappolin Creduto Principe	Cokain, Aston	(collection) 1658	1633	C4894
797	The Shepherd's Paradise	Montague, Walter	(27 Sept. 1658) 1659	1633	M2475
798	1 Sir Francis Drake	Davenant, William	20 Jan. 1659	1658	D327
799	The London Chanticleers	Anon.	28 Jan. 1659	1659	L2893
800	London's Triumph for Thomas Allen	Tatham, John	29 Oct. 1659	1659	T223
801	The Blind Beggar of Bednal Green	Chettle; Day (& Haughton?)	1659	1600	D464
802	Lady Alimony	Anon.	1659	1659	L162a
803	The Marriage of Oceanus and Britannia	Flecknoe, Richard	1659	1659	F1230a
804	The Noble Ingratitude	Lower, William	1659	1659	Q218
805	The World's Idol, Plutus	'H.H.B.'	1659	1659	A3686
806	The English Moor	Brome, Richard	(collection) 1659	1637	B4872
807	The Lovesick Court	Brome, Richard	(collection) 1659	1639	B4872
808	The Weeding of the Covent Garden	Brome, Richard	(collection) 1659	1632	B4872

GREG #	PLAY	AUTHOR	GREG DATE	H-S DATE	STC
809	The New Academy	Brome, Richard	(collection) 1659	1635	B4872
810	The Queen and Concubine	Brome, Richard	(collection) 1659	1635	B4872
811	The Sad One	Suckling, John	(collection) 1659	1637	S6130
812	Aminta	Dancer, John	(8 Nov. 1659) 1660	1660	T172
813	Andromana	'J.S.'	19 May 1660	1642	S3459
814	The Amorous Fantasm	Lower, William	1660	1660	Q215
815	The Mayor of Queenborough	Middleton, T.; (& Rowley, W.?)	13 Feb. 1661	1618	M1984
816	The City Night-Cap	Davenport, Robert	1661	1624	D369
817	A Cure for a Cuckold	Webster; Rowley, W. (& Heywood?)	1661	1625	W1220
818	Guy Earl of Warwick	Anon. ('B.J.' on t.p.)	1661	1593	J5

GREG #	PLAY	AUTHOR	GREG DATE	H-S DATE	STC
819	The Thracian Wonder	Anon. ('John Webster and William Rowley' on t.p. rejected)	1661	1599	T1078a
820	Tom Tyler and his Wife	Anon.	1661	1560	T1792
821	Anything for a Quiet Life	Middleton, T. (& Webster, J.?)	1662	1621	M1979
822	The Birth of Merlin	Rowley, W. (& another?; 'William Shakespeare and William Rowley' on t.p.)	1662	1608	R2096
823	The Jews' Tragedy	Hemming, William	1662	1626	H1425
824	Thorney Abbey	uncertain	(collection) 1662	uncertain	G1580
825	The Marriage Broker	uncertain	(collection) 1662	uncertain	G1580

GREG #	PLAY	AUTHOR	GREG DATE	H-S DATE	STC
826	Grim the Collier of Croydon	Haughton, William (revised for press by 'I.T.')	(collection) 1662	1600	G1580
827	2 The Siege of Rhodes	Davenant, William	1663	1659	D342
828	The Princess	Killigrew, Thomas	(collection) 1664	1636	K450
829	The Parson's Wedding	Killigrew, Thomas	(collection) 1664	1641	K450
830	Money is an Ass (Wealth Outwitted)	Jordan, Thomas	1668	1635	J1047
831	News from Plymouth	Davenant, William	(collection) 1673	1635	D320
832	The Distresses	Davenant, William	(collection) 1673	1639	D320
833	The Siege	Davenant, William	(collection) 1673	1629	D320
834	The Fair Favourite	Davenant, William	(collection) 1673	1638	D320
835	Gesta Grayorum [including The Masque of Proteus]	Bacon (?); Campion; Davison; etc.	1688	1594	C444
836	The Benefice	Wild, Robert	1689	1641	W2123

Section IV

Bibliography

Adkins, Mary Grace Muse. "The Genesis of Dramatic Satire Against the Puritan, as Illustrated in *A Knack to Know a Knave*," *RES*, 22(1946), 81–95.

_____. "Puritanism in the Plays and Pamphlets of Thomas Dekker," *Texas Studies in English*, 19(1939), 86–113.

Allen, Don Cameron. *The Star-Crossed Renaissance: The Quarrel About Astrology and Its Influence in England*. Durham: Duke University Press, 1941.

Ankenbrand, Karl. *Die Figur des Geistes in Drama die englischen Renaissance*. Naumberg: Lippert and Co., 1905.

Armstrong, W. A. "The Elizabethan Conception of the Tyrant," *RES*, 22(1946), 161–81.

Babb, Lawrence. *The Elizabethan Malady: A Study in Melancholia in English Literature from 1580–1642*. East Lansing: Michigan State University Press, 1951.

Barnhart, Thearle Aubrey. "An Index to the Characters in Caroline Drama." Unpublished dissertation, Ohio State University, 1945.

Bartley, James Orr. *Teague, Shenkin, and Sawney: Being an Historical Study of the Earliest Irish, Welsh, and Scottish Characters in English Plays*. Cork: Cork University Press, 1954.

Bentley, G. E. *The Jacobean and Caroline Stage*. 7 vols. Oxford: Clarendon Press, 1941–68.

Berlin, Normand. *The Base String: The Underworld in Elizabethan Drama*. Rutherford: Fairleigh Dickinson University Press, 1968.

Berndt, Elisa. *Dame Nature in der englischen Literatur bis herab zu Shakespeare*. Leipzeig: Mayer and Müller, 1923.

Bishop, William Warner. *A Checklist of American Copies of "Short-Title Catalogue" Books*. Ann Arbor: University of Michigan Press, 1950.

Black, Matthew. "Enter Citizens," in *Studies in the English Renaissance in Memory of Karl Julius Holzknecht*, ed. J.W. Bennett, O. Cargill, and V. Hall. New York: New York University Press, 1959, pp. 16–27.

Blaney, Glenn H. "Wardship in English Drama (1600–1650)," *SP*, 53(1956), 470–84.

Boughner, Daniel C. *The Braggart in Renaissance Comedy*. Minneapolis: University of Minnesota Press, 1954.

_____. "Vice, Braggart, and Falstaff," *Anglia*, 72(1954), 35–61.

Bowers, Fredson T. "The Audience and the Poisoners of Elizabethan Tradegy," *JEGP*, 36(1937), 491–504.

Brown, Louise. "The Portrayal of Spanish Characters in Selected Plays of the Elizabethan and Jacobean Eras: 1585–1625." Unpublished dissertation, Duke University, 1966.

Busby, Olive Mary. *Studies in the Development of the Fool in Elizabethan Drama*. London: Oxford University Press, 1923.

Camp, Charles W. *The Artisan in Elizabethan Literature*. New York: Columbia University Press, 1924.

Cardozo, D.L. *The Contemporary Jew In English Drama*. Amsterdam: H.J. Paris, 1925.

Cawley, Robert R. *Unpathed Waters: Studies in the Influence of the Voyagers on Elizabethan Literature*. Princeton: Princeton University Press, 1940.

————. *The Voyagers and Elizabethan Drama*. Boston: D.C. Heath, 1938.

Chambers, E.K. *The Elizabethan Stage*. 4 vols. Oxford: Clarendon Press, 1923.

Chapman, Raymond. "Fortune and Mutability in Renaissance Literature," *Cambridge Journal*, 5(1951–52), 374–82.

Chew, Samuel C. *The Crescent and the Rose: Islam and England during the Renaissance*. New York: Oxford University Press, 1937.

————. "Time and Fortune," *ELH*, 6(1939), 83–113.

Clough, Wilson O. "The Broken English of Foreign Characters of the Elizabethan Stage," *PQ*, 12(1933), 255–68.

Colby, Elbridge. *The Echo Device in Literature*. New York: New York Public Library, 1920.

Coleman, Edward D. *The Jew in English Drama: An Annotated Bibliography*. New York: New York Public Library and Ktav Publishing, 1968.

Crane, R.S. "The Vogue of Guy of Warwick from the Close of the Middle Ages to the Romantic Period," *PMLA*, 30(1915), 125–94.

Cushman, L.W. *The Devil and the Vice in English Dramatic Literature before Shakespeare*. Halle: Max Niemeyer, 1910.

Detlefsen, Hans. *Die Namengebung in den Dramen der Vorgänger Shakespeares*. Schleswig: Julius Bergas, 1914.

Duggan, G.C. *The Stage Irishman*. London: Longmans, Green and Co., 1937.

Eckhardt, Eduard. *Die Dialekt-und Ausländertypen des älteren englischen Dramas*. Louvain: A. Uystpruyst, 1910.

Erler, Ernst. *Die Namengebung bei Shakespeare*. Heidelberg: Carl Winter's Universititätsbuchhandlung, 1913.

Ewbank, Inga-Stina. " 'Those Pretty Devices': A Study of Masques in Plays," in *A Book of Masques in Honor of Allardyce Nicoll*, ed. T.J.B. Spencer. Cambridge: Cambridge University Press, 1967, pp. 407–48.

Feldman, Abraham B. "The Flemings in Shakespeare's Theatre," *N&Q*, 197(1952), 265–69.

————. "Netherlanders on the Early London Stage," *N&Q*, 196(1951), 333–35.

Fink, Z.S. "Jaques and the Malcontent Traveler," *PQ*, 14(1935), 237–52.

Fisch, Harold. *The Dual Image: A Study of the Figure of the Jew in English Literature*. London: Lincoln-Prager, 1959.

Gagen, Jean Elisabeth. *The New Woman: Her Emergence in English Drama, 1600–1730*. New York: Twayne, 1954.

Gilbert, Allan H. *The Symbolic Persons in the Masques of Ben Jonson*. Durham: Duke University Press, 1948.

Goldsmith, Robert H. "The Wild Man on the English Stage," *MLR*, 53(1958), 481–91.

————. *Wise Fools in Shakespeare*. East Lansing: Michigan State University Press, 1955.

Graves, Thornton S. "The Echo-Device," *MLN*, 36(1921), 120–21.

————. "Notes on Puritanism and the Stage," *SP*, 18(1921), 141–69.

Greenfield, Thelma N. *The Induction in Elizabethan Drama*. Eugene: University of Oregon Books, 1969.

Greg, W.W. *A Bibliography of the English Printed Drama to the Restoration*. 4 vols. London: The Bibliographical Society, 1939–59.

————. *The Shakespeare First Folio*. Oxford: Clarendon Press, 1955.

Harbage, Alfred. *Annals of English Drama, 975–1700,* revised by Samuel Schoenbaum. Philadelphia: University of Pennsylvania Press, 1964.

Harrison, Thomas P. "The Literary Background of Renaissance Poisons," *Texas Studies in English,* 27(1948), 35–67.

Hinze, Otto. *Studien zu Ben Jonson's Namengebung in seinen Dramen*. Leipzig: Thomas and Hubert, 1919.

Holzknecht, Karl J. *Outlines of Tudor and Stuart Plays*. New York: Barnes and Noble, 1959.

Honigmann, E.A.J. *The Stability of Shakespeare's Text*. Lincoln: University of Nebraska Press, 1965.

Houle, Peter J. *The English Morality and Related Drama: A Bibliographical Survey*. Hamden, Conn.: Archon Books, 1972.

Hughes, W.J. *Wales and the Welsh in English Literature*. London: Simpkin, Marshall, Hamilton, Kent, and Co., 1924.

Johansson, Bertil. *Law and Lawyers in Elizabethan England: As Evidenced in the Plays of Ben Jonson and Thomas Middleton*. Stockholm: Almguist and Wiksell, 1967.

Johnson, Francis R. *Astronomical Thought in Renaissance England: A Study of the English Scientific Writings from 1500 to 1645*. Baltimore: Johns Hopkins Press, 1937.

Jones, Eldred. *The Elizabethan Image of Africa*. Charlottesville: The University Press of Virginia, 1971.

————. *Othello's Countrymen*. London: Oxford University Press, 1965.

Jones, Robert C. "Italian Settings and the 'World' of Elizabethan Tragedy," *SEL,* 10(1970), 251–68.

Kellog, Allen B. "Nicknames and Nonce-Names in Shakespeare's Comedies," *Names,* 3(1955), 1–4.

Knowlton, E.C. "Genius as an Allegorical Figure," *MLN,* 39(1924), 89–95.

Landa, M.J. *The Jew in Drama*. London: P.S. King, 1926.

Leech, Clifford. "The Function of Locality in the Plays of Shakespeare and his Contemporaries," in *The Elizabethan Theatre,* ed. David Galloway. Toronto: Macmillan, 1969, pp. 103–16.

Levin, Harry. "Shakespeare's Nomenclature," in *Essays on Shakespeare,* ed. G.W. Chapman. Princeton: Princeton University Press, 1965, pp. 59–90.

Lyons, Bridget G. *Voices of Melancholy: Studies in Literary Treatments of Melancholy in Renaissance England*. London: Routledge and Kegan Paul, 1971.

McCullen, Joseph T. "Madness and the Isolation of Characters in Elizabethan and Early Stuart Drama," *SP,* 48(1951), 206–18.

————. "The Use of Parlor and Tavern Games in Elizabethan and Early Stuart Drama," *MLQ,* 14(1953), 7–14.

McCutchan, John Wilson. "Personified Abstractions as Characters in Elizabethan Drama." Unpublished dissertation, University of Virginia, 1949.

Mares, Francis H. "The Origin of the Figure Called 'The Vice' in Tudor Drama," *HLQ,* 22 (1958), 11–29.

Mason, John. *The Turke,* ed. J.Q. Adams. Louvain: A Uystprayst, 1913.

Maxfield, Ezra K. "The Quakers in English Stage Plays before 1800," *PMLA,* 45(1930), 256–73.

Bibliography

Maxwell, Baldwin. "The Hungry Knave in the Beaumont and Fletcher Plays," *PQ*, 5 (1926), 299–305.

Mehl, Dieter. *The Elizabethan Dumb Show*. Cambridge: Harvard University Press, 1966.

Michelson, H. *The Jew in Early English Literature*. Amsterdam: H.J. Paris, 1926.

Miles, Theodore. "Place Realism in a Group of Caroline Plays,"*RES*, 18(1942), 428–40.

Milligan, Burton. "The Roaring Boy in Tudor and Stuart Literature," *SAB*, 15(1941), 184–90.

Modder, Montagu Frank. *The Jew in the Literature of England to the End of the Nineteenth Century*. New York: Meridan Books, 1960.

Moore, John Robert. "The Tradition of Angelic Singing in English Drama," *JEGP*, 22 (1923), 89–99.

Myers, Aaron M. "Representation and Misrepresentation of the Puritan in Elizabethan Drama." Unpublished dissertation, University of Pennsylvania, 1931.

Nicoll, Allardyce. *Stuart Masks and the Renaissance Stage*. London: G. Harrap, 1937.

Niva, Weldon N. "Significant Character Names in English Drama to 1603." Unpublished dissertation, University of Pennsylvania, 1959.

Owen, A.L. *The Famous Druids*. Oxford: Clarendon Press, 1962.

Parr, Johnstone. *Tamburlaine's Malady and Other Essays on Astrology in Elizabethan Drama*. University: University of Alabama Press, 1953.

Peake, Richard H. "The Stage Prostitute in English Dramatic Tradition from 1558–1625." Unpublished dissertation, University of Georgia, 1967.

Pearson, Lu Emily. "Elizabethan Widows," in *Stanford Studies in Language and Literature*, ed. H. Craig. Stanford: Stanford University Press, 1941, pp. 124–42.

Peery, William. "The Roaring Boy Again," *SAB*, 23(1948), 12–16, 78–86.

Perkinson, R.H. "Topographical Comedy in the Seventeenth Century," *ELH*, 3(1936), 270–90.

Pollard, A.W. and G.R. Redgrave. *A Short-Title Catalogue of Books Printed in England, Scotland, and Ireland and of English Books Printed Abroad, 1475–1640*. London: The Bibliographical Society, 1926.

Power, William. "Middleton's Way with Names," *N&Q*, 205(1960), 26–29, 56–60, 136–40, 175–79.

Pratt, S.M. "Antwerp and the Elizabethan Mind," *MLQ*, 24(1963), 53–60.

Quinn, David B. *The Elizabethans and the Irish*. Ithaca: Cornell University Press, 1966.

Reed, Robert R. *Bedlam on the Jacobean Stage*. Cambridge: Harvard University Press, 1952.

––––––. *The Occult on the Tudor and Stuart Stage*. Boston: Christopher House, 1965.

Rice, Warner G. "Turk, Moor, and Persian in English Literature from 1550–1600, with Particular Reference to the Drama." Unpublished dissertation, Harvard University, 1927.

Rosenberg, Edgar. *From Shylock to Svengali: Jewish Stereotypes in English Fiction*. Stanford: Stanford University Press, 1960.

––––––. *The Jew in Western Drama: An Essay and a Check List*. New York: New York Public Library and Ktav Publishing, 1968.

Russell, H.K. "Tudor and Stuart Dramatizations of the Doctrine of Natural and Moral Philosophy," *SP*, 31(1934), 1–27.

Schelling, Felix E. "Some Features of the Supernatural as Represented in Plays of the Reigns of Elizabeth and James," *MP*, 1(1903), 31–47.

Schoenbaum, Samuel. *Annals of English Drama, 975–1700: A Second Supplement to the Revised Edition*. Evanston: Department of English of Northwestern University, 1970.

––––––. *Annals of English Drama, 975–1700: Supplement to the Revised Edition*. Evanston: Department of English of Northwestern University, 1966.

Bibliography

Scott, Florence R. "Teg: The Stage Irishman," *MLR*, 42(1947), 314–20.

Scrimgeour, James. "The 'Ougly Shape': Despair in Early English Drama," *Massachusetts Studies in English*, 1(1968), 75–87.

Silvette, Herbert. *The Doctor on the Stage: Medicine and Medical Men in Seventeenth-Century England*, ed. Francelia Butler. Knoxville: University of Tennessee Press, 1967.

Spencer, Theodore. "The Elizabethan Malcontent," in *Joseph Quincy Adams Memorial Studies*, ed. James G. McManaway, Giles Dawson, and E.E. Willoughby. Washington: The Folger Shakespeare Library, 1948, pp. 523–35.

Starnes, D.T. "The Figure Genius in the Renaissance," *SRen*, 11(1964), 234–44.

Stokes, Francis Griffin. *A Dictionary of the Characters and Proper Names in Shakespeare*. London: George G. Harrap, 1924.

Stoner, Arthur B. "The Usurer in Elizabethan Drama," *PMLA*, 31(1916), 190–210.

Sugden, E.H. *A Topographical Dictionary to the Works of Shakespeare and His Fellow Dramatists*. Manchester: Manchester University Press, 1925.

Swain, Barbara. *Fools and Folly During the Middle Ages and the Renaissance*. New York: Columbia University Press, 1932.

Thompson, Elbert N.S. *The Controversy Between the Puritans and the Stage*. New York: Henry Holt, 1903.

Thomson, W.H. *Shakespeare's Characters: A Historical Dictionary*. New York: British Book Centre, 1951.

Treneer, Anne. *The Sea in English Literature from Beowulf to Donne*. Liverpool: Liverpool University Press, 1926.

Van der Speck, Cornelis. *The Church and the Churchman in English Dramatic Literature before 1642*. Amsterdam: H.J. Paris, 1930.

Vandiver, Edward P. "The Elizabethan Dramatic Parasite," *SP*, 32(1935), 411–27.

Walbridge, Earle F. "Drames à Clef: A List of Plays with Characters Based on Real People," *New York Public Library Bulletin*, 60(1956), 156–74.

Watson, Harold F. *The Sailor in English Fiction and Drama, 1550–1800*. New York: Columbia University Press, 1931.

Watt, Homer A., Karl J. Holzknecht, and Raymond Ross. *Outlines of Shakespeare's Plays*. New York: Barnes and Noble, 1969.

Weaver, Charles P. *The Hermit in English Literature from the Beginnings to 1660*. Nashville: George Peabody College for Teachers, 1924.

Welsford, Enid. *The Court Masque*. Cambridge: Cambridge University Press, 1927.

_____. *The Fool: His Social and Literary History*. London: Faber and Faber, 1935.

West, Robert H. *The Invisible World*. Athens: University of Georgia Press, 1939.

Wheeler, Charles F. *Classical Mythology in the Plays, Masques, and Poems of Ben Jonson*. Princeton: Princeton University Press, 1938.

Wiley, Autrey Nell. "The English Vogue of Prologues and Epilogues," *MLN*, 47(1932), 255–57.

_____. "Female Prologues and Epilogues in English Plays," *PMLA*, 48(1933), 1060–79.

Wing, Donald. *A Short-Title Catalogue of Books Printed in England, Scotland, Ireland, Wales, and British America and of English Books Printed in Other Countries, 1641–1700*. 3 vols. New York: The Index Society, 1945–51.

Withington, Robert. "Braggart, Devil, and 'Vice'," *Speculum*, 11(1936), 124–29.

_____. "The Development of the 'Vice'," in *Essays in Memory of Barrett Wendell*, ed. W.R. Castle and Paul Kaufman. Cambridge: Harvard University Press, 1926, pp. 155–67.

_____. " 'Vice' and 'Parasite': A Note on the Evolution of the Elizabethan Villain," *PMLA*, 49(1934), 743–51.

Wright, Celeste T. "The Amazons in Elizabethan Literature," *SP*, 37(1940), 433–56.

———. "Some Conventions Regarding the Usurer in Elizabethan Literature," *SP*, 31(1934), 176–97.

———. "The Usurer's Sin in Elizabethan Literature," *SP*, 35(1938), 178–94.

Wright, Louis B. "Animal Actors on the English Stage before 1642," *PMLA*, 42(1927), 656–69.

———. "Madmen as Vaudeville Performers on the Elizabethan Stage," *JEGP*, 30(1931), 48–54.

Yearsley, Macleod. *Doctors in Elizabethan Drama*. London: John Bale, Sons, and Danielsson, 1933.

Young, Steven C. "A Check List of Tudor and Stuart Induction Plays," *PQ*, 48(1969), 131–34.